TWENTIETH CENTURY
INTERPRETATIONS
Maynard Mack, *Series Editor*
Yale University

NOW AVAILABLE
Collections of Critical Essays
ON

The Adventures of Huckleberry Finn

The Frogs

The Great Gatsby

Hamlet

Henry V

The Iceman Cometh

Samson Agonistes

The Sound and the Fury

Twelfth Night

Walden

TWENTIETH CENTURY INTERPRETATIONS
OF

ALL FOR LOVE

TWENTIETH CENTURY INTERPRETATIONS
OF

ALL FOR LOVE

A Collection of Critical Essays

Edited by
BRUCE KING

Prentice-Hall, Inc.　A SPECTRUM BOOK　*Englewood Cliffs, N. J.*

To Nicole

Contents

PART TWO—*View Points*

Introduction

by Bruce King

John Dryden was born August 9, 1631, at Aldwinckle, Northamptonshire; his parents were landed gentry, and he was the eldest of fourteen children. He was educated first at Westminster School and later (1650-54) at Trinity College, Cambridge. His first important poem was an elegy on the death of Oliver Cromwell (1659); a year later he published *Astræa Redux* on the restoration of Charles II to the throne. Both poems probably reflect the majority opinion of their day—they are concerned with the need for stability and order in the country after the anarchy and changing governments which followed the execution of Charles I.

After the Restoration Dryden began to establish a reputation among London literary and intellectual society. He was elected, in 1662, a fellow of the newly founded Royal Society for the development of the arts and sciences, but he soon let his membership lapse. Numerous allusions in his plays and poetry show a familiarity with the new scientific ideas of the age. In his *Ode to Charleton* (1662) he draws an implied analogy between the restoration of Charles to the throne and the restoration of knowledge to England after the supposed dark ages of scholastic thought. His first play, *The Wild Gallant*, was acted in 1663, and in the same year he married Lady Elizabeth Howard, the sister of Sir Robert Howard. The first of Dryden's three children, Charles, was born in 1666. Dryden wrote *The Indian Queen* (1664), one of the first heroic plays, in collaboration with Sir Robert Howard. This was followed by *The Indian Emperour* (1665). The next year he wrote *Annus Mirabilis*, a long poem meant to counter the fears of certain Protestants that recent naval disasters and the fire which swept London were signs of divine disapproval of the government. *An Essay of Dramatic Poesy* (1668) is a charming conversation piece in which the relative merits of ancient, modern, English, and French drama are debated. Besides offering us a useful compendium of the various critical theories with which a seventeenth-century dramatist had to contend, the *Essay* is of interest as an example of Dryden's sceptical, undogmatic personality. Soon he was created Poet Laureate (1668) and afterwards became Historiographer Royal (1670). Dryden inherited

1

a private income, and his official position entitled him to a small pension, although it was seldom paid; he was sufficiently well-off, however, that in 1667 he loaned five hundred pounds to Charles II.

The two parts of *The Conquest of Granada*, the most extravagant of his bombastic heroic plays (performed in 1670 and 1671), led to Dryden's being ridiculed in *The Rehearsal* (1671), a parody by Buckingham and others of literary fashions of the time. Dryden later said that when he wrote such plays he knew they were bad enough to please, and it is probable that they were written with a sense of ironic detachment. He soon tired of heroicism. *Marriage à la Mode* (1672) is his best comedy. It blends the new comedy of manners with the older situational comedy, and is rich with social observation and witty dialogue. Dryden's ability to portray the fashionable, the clever, and the unscrupulous was aided by his familiarity with the young, sophisticated wits who attended the court of Charles II. *Marriage à la Mode* is dedicated to John Wilmot, Earl of Rochester, the most brilliant of the young wits, an excellent poet in his own right, and a leader of fashionable society. In the preface to *The Assignation* (1673), addressed to Sir Charles Sedley, also a poet, wit, and one of the intimate circle of young courtiers, Dryden wrote:

> We have . . . our genial nights, where our discourse is neither too serious, nor too light, but always pleasant, and for the most part instructive: the raillery neither too sharp upon the present, nor too censorious on the absent; and the cups only such as will raise the conversation of the night, without disturbing the business of the morrow.

Since the wits were famous for their debauchery, Dryden perhaps exaggerates the moderation of such evenings.

Aureng-Zebe (1675) is the last and best of Dryden's plays in the heroic style; significantly, the characterization, language, and emotions are less extravagant than before, and look forward to the more natural style of *All for Love* (1677). The virtuous conduct of Aureng-Zebe may have been influenced by the growing popularity of Racine's plays among the courtiers; however, as the preface to *All for Love* shows, Dryden soon decided that such idealized virtue has no place in serious drama. *The State of Innocence* (1677) is a rhymed operatic version of Milton's *Paradise Lost*. Milton was not fashionable during the Restoration, and Dryden was one of the few critics of the time who recognized his achievement. Echoes of Milton's verse in Dryden's poems and plays, and allusions to Milton in Dryden's criticism, show that he was aware of a competitor who was accomplishing something more serious than the popular writers of the age.

The Roman Catholics were accused in 1678 of plotting to assassinate Charles II with the aim of putting his brother James on the throne.

Soon England was on the verge of civil war; Shaftesbury used the supposed Popish Plot as an excuse to bar James' right to succession and to replace him with Monmouth, one of Charles' illegitimate sons. While the mass of the population probably hoped only to exclude a Roman Catholic from the throne, Shaftesbury and his followers intended to use the crisis to attempt to weaken the powers of the king, and, eventually, to establish a republic or elective monarchy. Dryden, who saw the crisis as a threat to the established laws of England, wrote pamphlets and poems in support of the court. *Absalom and Achitophel* (1681) is a mock-epic poem, using the heroic style to satirize Shaftesbury and his followers. By using biblical allusions and echoes of *Paradise Lost,* Dryden treats Shaftesbury as a satanic figure and Monmouth as a false Messiah who have tried to tempt England into disobedience to its divinely appointed king. The poem is rich in imagery, implied analogies, and imitations of other poets; it is one of the best things Dryden ever wrote. *The Medal* (1682) is another verse satire on Shaftesbury. In the same year Dryden published *MacFlecknoe,* a humorous, good-natured mock-heroic poem, at the expense of Shadwell, a writer on the side of the political opposition.

Religio Laici (1682) is the first of Dryden's major religious poems. In it he adopts the position of a middle-of-the-road Anglican, sceptical of the claims made for rational religion by the Deists and other intellectuals of the age, distrustful of Rome's claim to temporal authority, and opposed to the fuss made over minor points of religious dogma and ceremony by the Protestant Non-Conformists. Faced by the inability of any church, philosophy, or sect to offer a sure guide to God's wishes, Dryden aligns himself with the established church and advises others to do so if England is to avoid continual religious strife.

After the death of Charles II in 1685, James II continued Dryden in his offices as Poet Laureate and Historiographer Royal. On January 19, 1686, Dryden was observed going to Catholic mass. While the reasons for his conversion to Rome are obscure, they appear to be sincere. In later years he resisted offers by the next government to change his religion, and he suffered financially and through censorship for his beliefs. In a letter dated November 7, 1699, he wrote:

> The Court rather speaks kindly of me, than does anything for me, though they promise largely; and perhaps they think I will advance, as they go backward: in which they will be much deceived: for I can never go an Inch beyond my Conscience and my Honour. If they will consider me as a Man, who have done my best to improve the Language, and Especially the Poetry, and will be content with my acquiescence under the present Government, and forbearing satire on it, that I can promise, because I can perform it: but I can neither take the

Oaths, nor forsake my Religion, because I know not what Church to go to, if I leave the Catholique; they are all so divided amongst themselves in matter of faith, necessary to Salvation: and yet all assuming the name of Protestants. May God be pleased to open your Eyes, as he has opened mine: Truth is but one; and they who have once heard of it, can plead no Excuse, if they do not embrace it. But these things are too serious, for a trifling Letter.

Dryden's conversion may have resulted from his study of theology or it may have been based on a visionary experience.[1] In either case his adherence to Rome probably was influenced by the desire to find some authority to prevent or limit excesses of private opinion in religious thought. Participating in national politics, he was well aware of the tendency of seventeenth-century Protestants to split into numerous factions. Such splinter groups seemed to threaten the government, the national church, and established society; and, as recent history had shown, the dissenters could never form a stable government. *The Hind and the Panther* (1687), an unusual poem combining a beast fable, medieval allegory, satire, and Restoration wit, discusses political and theological problems in treating the comparative arguments for the Anglican and Roman churches. Anglicanism is seen as a poor compromise which, in trying to be inclusive of so many factions, leads to further confusion and dissent.

In his attempt to strengthen the Roman Catholic position in England, James II alienated the high Tories and the Church of England bishops who had previously viewed the monarchy as a shield against Non-Conformity and political radicalism. At the invitation of both Whig and Tory leaders, William of Orange invaded England in November, 1688, and received wide support. James II lost his nerve and fled to France. The throne was declared vacant and a special Parliament appointed William and Mary as joint monarchs. Dryden refused to take the required oaths supporting the new government and lost his offices of Poet Laureate and Historiographer Royal. Although he still owned his family estates in Northamptonshire and Wiltshire, he found it necessary to supplement his income by again writing for the stage. *Don Sebastian* (1689) is his only tragedy which is often ranked with *All for Love*. The characterization of *Don Sebastian* is more lifelike than in most of Dryden's plays, and through the plot and imagery we are reminded of such deeper matters as original sin and man's duties in this world:

> Nor has a Christian privilege to dye.
> Alas thou art too young in thy new Faith:

[1] See *The Hind and the Panther*, II, line 658: "I saw myself the lambent easy light."

> *Brutus* and *Cato* might discharge their Souls,
> And give 'em Furlo's for another World:
> But we, like Centry's, are oblig'd to stand
> In starless Nights, and wait the pointed hour.
> > *Don Sebastian,* II, i.

While some of Dryden's best poems—including *Alexander's Feast,* the Purcell Ode, and the verse epistle to his cousin, John Driden— were written after the Revolution, his main effort went into translations of Juvenal, Persius (1693), and Virgil (1697). Previously, English translations were either dull and pedantic or so bold in their freedom that the original meaning was lost. Dryden, as Johnson said, fixed "the limits of poetical liberty," and gave us "just rules and examples of translation." Dryden turned down suggestions that he dedicate his *Aeneid* to King William, and it seems probable that he remained a secret Jacobite, silently hoping for the return of the Stuarts to the throne. Dryden died on May 1, 1700. He was buried in the Poet's Corner at Westminster Abbey. His last verse was the "Secular Masque," contributed to Vanbrugh's adaptation of Fletcher's *The Pilgrim,* in which he commented upon the political and social changes of the preceding age:

> All, all of a piece throughout
> Thy chase had a beast in view;
> Thy wars brought nothing about;
> Thy lovers were all untrue.
> 'T is well an old age is out,
> And time to begin a new.

All for Love (1677) is one of the few English tragedies written between the mid-seventeenth and late nineteenth centuries which still commands critical attention. While it was seldom performed during Dryden's lifetime, it has steadily gained in popularity; during our century it has often been seen on the university and professional stage.

The story of Antony and Cleopatra had been treated of course by English dramatists previous to Dryden, but not in the same way. Shakespeare's *Antony and Cleopatra,* for example, contains a wide-ranging mixture of scepticism, irony, and grandeur. Dryden's play is smaller in scope, more polished, and has a different theme. It is a study of the psychology of love and holds up for our inspection the emotions of two people who, having found satisfaction together, are threatened by moral obligations and society. Dryden depicts an idealized love; his theme is neither the deep, one-sided passions of lust portrayed in *Antony and Cleopatra,* nor the refined, spiritual love portrayed in many seventeenth-century plays. The story shows the varying pressures on Antony's affections and on the decisions that he makes. The plot has a pendular motion as Antony oscillates from one allegiance to another. Love, war, empire, friendship, family, and wife make their appeals to Antony. He recognizes the justice of each claim, and after each confrontation he temporarily accepts the point of view offered, but he finally chooses to live with and die for Cleopatra. Each important character may be said to be representative of some value, such as honor (Ventidius), friendship (Dollabella), and family (the children); each act is designed to illustrate Antony's attachment to and eventual rejection of such values for the sake of his love.

The design of *All for Love* contributes towards the idealization of emotion into its pure state. The suicide of Ventidius shows the depth of his friendship; it is a noble act, but is of lesser value than the love which Antony has found in Cleopatra. Cleopatra's rejection of the offers made to her by Caesar demonstrates the purity of her love and makes her worth Antony's sacrifice of the world. Her suicide shows Roman courage, symbolically bringing together Roman and Egyptian values. The eunuch Alexas might be said to offer the most complete contrast to Antony. His jealousy of Antony's potency provides a center of psychological interest for the reader, and his attempt to save his own skin sharply contrasts with Antony's decision to die for Cleopatra. While Antony has all the world if he leaves Cleopatra, Alexas has nothing of worth, except his life. He is completely despiritualized, yet it is his intervention which causes the final tragedy.

It is only necessary to compare the steadfast love of Antony and Cleopatra with the conduct of others in the play to see how strongly our sympathies are directed towards them. Caesar is cold, passionless, and a coward; emotionally he is an Alexas with an army at his command. Octavia, though noble, is also cold, and there is perhaps a little of the shrew in her character. Judged, however, by Roman values, Octavia is admirable. She is even capable of forgiving Antony, but is otherwise limited. Dollabella, though Antony's best friend, easily succumbs to the temptation to supplant Antony in Cleopatra's affections. Although it is true that he loved Cleopatra in the past, and that similarities between his character and Antony's make a similar choice of mistress probable, his attempt to seduce Cleopatra is still dereliction from his duties as a friend. An even more interesting study of personality is presented to us in Ventidius. While he remains constant to his Roman values throughout the play, the limitations of such ideals eventually corrupt his honesty. He begins by disapproving of Antony's lapse from Roman virtue, but ends by cooperating with corrupt Alexas to deceive the lovers. While Alexas and Ventidius have different aims, they temporarily reach the same level of dishonesty.

In *All for Love* the characters often criticize each other's language. The play begins with a bombastic prophecy by the priest Serapion; this is mocked by Alexas. At least thirteen times during the course of the play characters comment upon the imagery, rhetorical style, or tone others use. While such questioning of false rhetoric is appropriate to a play in which the hero and heroine's deaths are brought about by duplicity and a succession of lies, it also implies a concern with the relation of language to truth. The language we use embodies the values of our culture. But what happens when we feel or perceive something of value beyond commonly accepted cultural standards? This is Antony's problem. Through his sensual delight in Cleopatra he has discovered love of more value than Roman ideals. But just as the eunuch Alexas is physically debarred from knowing love, so Antony lacks a vocabulary permitting the valuation of love over Roman duty. When Ventidius and Octavia appeal to his sense of honor and family, Antony temporarily accepts the values involved, but he need only see Cleopatra to realize that their love is more valuable than anything he could gain by redeeming his fortunes. The meeting between Octavia and Cleopatra illustrates this opposition of values. Octavia considers Cleopatra little better than a trollop, whereas Cleopatra scorns the frigid, dutiful love, legitimatized by society, which Octavia represents. But Cleopatra has no culturally acceptable means to defend the nature of her love, which is neither mere Egyptian sensuality nor stern Roman virtue. In a later scene we see her lamenting that fate has deprived her of a lawful relationship with Antony. Throughout the play it is asked whether Antony and Cleopatra are honest in their love, or whether it is merely a combination of lust, infatuation, self-interest, and dotage. Their deaths prove, and therefore symbolically legitimatize, their love.

The imagery of *All for Love* is appropriate to its theme. Throughout the play Rome is associated with images of coolness, reason, warfare, manliness, and duty, while Egypt is associated with images of night, heat, sensuality, allurement, and effeminacy. But unlike the grand contrast between Roman and Egyptian qualities in Shakespeare's play, the imagistic opposition in *All for Love* is less important and the contrast is blurred. An atmosphere of grey, decaying grandeur is appropriate to a story concerned with the last stages of Antony's life, when all the world has been sacrificed for love. Images of grandeur, the world, and space consequently are found side by side with images of decay, ruin, age, and the passing of time.

Even more important, Dryden uses imagery to define the point of view of the speaker. If Shakespeare's imagery has similarities with the expanded analogies of lyric poetry, Dryden's imagery, which reflects a character's point of view, looks forward to later novelistic techniques. Dryden uses imagery as it is applicable to each specific situation rather than to create expanding patterns. As Moody Prior points out,[2] whenever Ventidius speaks of Cleopatra he uses words suggestive of tainted allurements ("gaudy slaughter," "poisoned gifts," "infected"), whereas in Antony's speeches Cleopatra appears in imagery free from any suggestion of taint. From Ventidius' point of view, Cleopatra and Egypt represent "lascivious hours," whereas Charmion sees the Romans as "iron statues."

All for Love is a socially subversive play. While recognizing social obligations, it challenges their omnipotence by holding up for our admiration an unlawful but fully achieved love. Dr. Johnson was well aware of the radical moral nature of *All for Love:* "it has one fault equal to many, though rather moral than critical, that by admitting the romantic omnipotence of love, [Dryden] has recommended as laudable and worthy of imitation that conduct which, through all ages, the good have censured as vicious and the bad despised as foolish." Johnson's comment, with its awareness that Dryden was recommending neither the values of conventional marriage nor the libertine indulgence of the flesh, is one of the best interpretations of the play.

The success of *All for Love* hinges on Dryden's ability to convince us of the fulfillment Antony found with Cleopatra. On the whole he is convincing. Some of Antony's speeches offer us a pure distillation of mature love unmixed with any lesser emotions:

> How I lov'd
> Witness ye Dayes and Nights, and all your hours,
> That Danc'd away with Down upon your Feet,
> As all your business were to count my passion.
> One day past by, and nothing saw but Love;
> Another came, and still 'twas only Love:
> The Suns were weary'd out with looking on,
> And I untyr'd with loving.
> I saw you ev'ry day, and all the day;
> And ev'ry day was still but as the first:
> So eager was I still to see you more.

Other speeches picture the fullness of love:

> Think we have had a clear and glorious day;
> And Heav'n did kindly to delay the Storm

[2] Cf. Moody E. Prior, "Tragedy and the Heroic Play," in *Dryden: A Collection of Critical Essays*, ed. Bernard Schelling (Englewood Cliffs: Prentice-Hall, 1963), pp. 95-114.

Just till our close of Ev'ning. Ten years love,
And not a moment lost, but all improv'd
To th' utmost Joys: What Ages have we liv'd?
And now to die each others; and, so dying,
While hand in hand we walk in Groves below,
Whole Troops of Lovers Ghosts shall flock about us,
And all the Train be ours.

Some speeches seem sentimental and almost adolescent in the feelings they represent. The following passage mars, but does not ruin, Dryden's play:

Go; leave me, Soldier;
(For you're no more a Lover:) leave me dying:
Push me all pale and panting from your bosome,
And, when your March begins, let one run after
Breathless almost for Joy; and cry, she's dead:
The Soldiers shout; you then perhaps may sigh,
And muster all your *Roman* Gravity;
Ventidius chides; and strait your Brow cleares up:
As I had never been.

Antony's melancholy and tears are overdone. The conversation between Cleopatra and Dollabella is too reminiscent of the seduction scenes of Restoration comedy, although it is possible Dryden meant it to be so. The final speech of the play is awkward and sentimentalized:

See, see how the Lovers sit in State together,
As they were giving Laws to half Mankind.
Th' impression of a smile left in her face,
Shows she dy'd pleas'd with him for whom she liv'd,
And went to charm him in another World.

Dryden seems at times less poised than we might expect from such a craftsman. But if *All for Love* has faults—and it does—they are minor in comparison to its total effect.

All for Love is supposedly the only play that Dryden wrote for himself. Although it shares several characteristics with the new sentimental drama developing in the mid-1670s, it represents a radical departure from Dryden's previous work. The major form of English drama after the restoration of Charles II to the throne in 1660 was the heroic play, an attempt to turn the Renaissance epic into theatre. The heroic play was usually written in rhymed heroic couplets and was notable for its exotic settings, larger than life characters, violent action, extravagant speeches, variety of character, and overriding concern with questions of valor, honor, and other highly stylized forms of noble

conduct. In *Tyrannic Love* (1669) and *The Conquest of Granada*
(1670) Dryden carried the heroic play to new heights of violence and
extravagant behavior. Although such plays were fashionable and in
great demand, it is probable that Dryden had his tongue in his cheek
while writing them and that they were seen in a humorous light by
the more sophisticated members of his audience. It is not surprising
that Dryden wearied of the heroic style and began to search for a
more natural, more serious form of drama.

Before writing *All for Love* Dryden had already transferred his
allegiance to a set of critical principles opposed to those upon which
the heroic play was based. In his prologue to *Aureng-Zebe* (published
1676) Dryden confessed that "he has now another taste of wit" and
has grown "weary of his long-loved mistress, rhyme." Dryden was
aware that the artificiality of the heroic play represented a severe
limitation. He also confessed: "Passion's too fierce to be in fetters
bound, / And Nature flies him like enchanted ground . . . A secret
shame / Invades his breast at Shakespeare's sacred name."

If English drama was to take a new direction, in what direction
should it go? Previously the heroic play had imitated the Corneillean
hero who, although not consistently virtuous, was admirable for his
physical prowess and noble actions. During the 1670s English drama
was influenced by the growing popularity of Racine in France. The
Restoration courtiers, always up-to-date in their appreciation of French
fashion, were supplied with plays in which, as in Dryden's *Aureng-
Zebe,* the hero illustrated a pattern of almost blameless conduct. But
Dryden soon moved on from the imitation of French drama and, as
shown by his attack on Racine in the preface to *All for Love,* decided
that tragedy should hold up for compassion a criminal love.

The most influential English critic of the day was Thomas Rymer,
whose *Tragedies of the Last Age Considered* taught the necessity of
poetic justice in drama. According to Rymer the task of tragedy was
to illustrate moral truths; good should be rewarded, evil punished.
Rymer, for example, condemned Shakespeare's *Othello* for showing a
world in which evil seemed unchecked by divine intervention. While
it is easy to mock Rymer's theory of poetic justice, such views were
common to medieval and Renaissance criticism. Neo-classical criticism
had no way of justifying drama in which characters develop outside
a moral framework, and offer convincing alternative moral and religious views to those accepted by society. While Renaissance epic
theory permitted admiration for valiant if ethically erratic heroes,
Dryden in *All for Love* goes beyond Renaissance critical theory in
creating pity for a hero who, for the sake of love, eventually rejects
all social obligation.

At a time when Rymer claimed that plot, decorum of manners, and poetic justice were the most important aspects of drama, Dryden found an alternative theory of tragedy in Rapin's *Réflexions sur la poétique d'Aristote* (1674). According to Rapin (as interpreted by Dryden), the purpose of tragedy is to raise pity and compassion for the faults of the hero. The emotions raised in the audience towards the protagonist are of more importance than the formal structure of the drama. But how are the emotions to be raised? Dryden's notes, written as a reply to Rymer's *Tragedies of the Last Age Considered,* provide the answer:

> Rapin attributes more to the *dictio,* that is, to the words and discourses of a tragedy, than Aristotle had done, who places them in the last rank of beauties; perhaps only last in order, because they are the last product of the design, of the disposition or connection of its parts; of the characters, of the manners of those characters, and of the thoughts proceeding from those manners.
>
> Rapin's words are remarkable: " 'Tis not the admirable intrigue, the surprising events, the extraordinary incidents that make the beauty of a tragedy; 'tis the discourses when they are natural and passionate."
>
> So are Shakespeare's.

Rapin offered a justification for Dryden's replacing the heroic couplet with the Shakespearean-influenced blank verse of *All for Love.* Rapin also wrote that while pity and terror may in the past have been the mainsprings of drama, love is now the passion "which most predominates in our souls." Whereas Dryden's heroic plays had been concerned with the rise and fall of empires, the deeds of warriors, and displays of artificial, idealized conduct, *All for Love* shows that love is the passion which "most predominates in our souls."

Dryden's decision to use blank verse in *All for Love* indicates a fundamental change of attitude towards his material, especially towards his characters. Whereas the heroes of the rhymed verse plays were held up for admiration (or, as I believe, for our sophisticated laughter), Antony and Cleopatra earn our sympathy. We do not judge the hero and heroine. Their actions seem inevitable and correct. At the play's conclusion they receive our pity, and their passion is vindicated by the depth of feeling and nobility shown through their deaths.

Dryden makes our response to Antony and Cleopatra pitying and compassionate by pointing to their nobler and softer qualities. Myris says that Antony dreams out his hours; Alexas says that Cleopatra "dotes, She dotes . . . on this vanquish'd Man." Antony "eats not, drinks not, sleeps not, has no use / Of any thing, but thought;" "He censures eagerly his own misdeeds." He observes his birthday with "double pomp of sadness." Ventidius finds this "mournful, wondrous mournful!" and comments: "How sorrow shakes him! / So, now the Tempest tears him up by th' Roots, / And on the ground extends the noble ruin." When Ventidius and Antony meet, the former weeps: "This is no common Deaw, / I have not wept this forty year." When Ventidius upbraids his passion for Cleopatra, Antony replies that "She deserves / More Worlds than I can lose."

If the loves of Antony and Cleopatra represent a higher value than any other in the play, why does Dryden's preface say that he wrote the play for the excellency of its moral? "For the chief persons represented, were famous patterns of unlawful love; and their end accordingly was unfortunate." *All for Love* does not picture criminal love deservedly punished for its sins; rather it illustrates a transcendent love for which the world is well lost. Dryden was fully aware that *All for Love* flouted current critical tastes in portraying a genuine tension between conventional morals and some private emotion, such as love. If Dryden contradicts himself by saying that *All for Love* illustrates a moral, it is probably because Rymer's book had just been published and was highly influential among the courtiers. Dryden's preface deviously pretends that *All for Love* does in fact illustrate a moral; having given the slip to his critics, he then, under the guise of attacking French drama, rejects Rymer's claim that the characters in a play must always act nobly and with decorum.[3]

All for Love lacks an involved moral intelligence which judges the actions and emotions of the hero and heroine. This once seemed to me a limitation when compared with the critical pressure we can feel operating through Dryden's other plays and satires. But I now feel that such a judgment must be modified in that it demands from Dryden's play something totally opposed to his purpose. Dryden, like most of the great Augustan satirists, was suspicious of romantic feelings. He usually portrayed men as self-seeking and egotistical, deluded by vain fancies, and only saved from worse corruption by the limitations imposed by society and religion on the indulgence of emotion. In *All for Love* Dryden ignores the pessimistic view of human nature common to the Augustan conservative tradition. Instead he depicts a love which, although neglecting social obligations, rises above selfishness and corruption. Perhaps the best way to show the difference in attitude between *All for Love* and the heroic plays is to compare a few passages from each. In the heroic plays love is represented as farcical jealousy:

[3] For other influences on Dryden's preface, see Bruce King, "Dryden's Intent in *All for Love*," *College English*, XXIV (1963), 267-71.

> Who dares touch her I love? I'm all o'er love:
> Nay, I am Love; Love shot, and shot so fast,
> He shot himself into my breast at last.
>
> > I, *The Conquest of Granada,* III, i

Heroic love is also represented as wild imaginings, sensual desire, and
fulfilment of such excess that it borders on comedy:

> Oh, I could stifle you, with eager haste!
> Devour your kisses with my hungry taste!
> Rush on you! eat you! wander o'er each part,
> Raving with pleasure, snatch you to my heart!
> Then hold you off and gaze! then, with new rage,
> Invade you, till my conscious Limbs presage
> Torrents of joy, which all their banks o'erflow!
> So lost, so blest, as I but then could know!
>
> > *Aureng-Zebe,* IV, i

In *All for Love* Dryden excludes any humorous element in Antony's
descriptions of Cleopatra:

> There's no satiety of Love in thee;
> Enjoy'd, thou still art new; perpetual Spring
> Is in thy armes; the ripen'd fruit but falls,
> And blossoms rise to fill its empty place;
> And I grow rich by giving.

It is possible that our age, steeped in the ambiguities of human behavior disclosed by Freud and Dostoievsky, will not find *All for Love*
fully satisfying. The intense subjectivity of Donne's poetry with its
attempt to delineate particular feelings may seem preferable to Dryden's more generalized reflections upon love. We are more interested
in complex psychological states, such as Shakespeare's Egyptian bitch-
goddess, than in Dryden's simplification of problems into neat cate-
gories of love versus duty. It would be unfortunate if this were so.
All for Love offers an unusually fine example of the distillation of
emotions, with all impurities removed, arranged into a formal dramatic pattern. The over-all effect is closer to the warmly colored, clear
abstract designs in a painting of Mondrian or Rothko than the ex-
pressionism often found in modern drama. There is a classical economy of emotion and detail which will be appreciated by those who
are concerned with art for its own qualities rather than as a mirror
of contemporary anxieties.

PART ONE

Essays

Dryden and Shakespeare

by John Bailey

The fashion of making literary parallels, for contrast or comparison, is one that has rather passed away. Homer and Virgil, the *Iliad* and the *Odyssey, Paradise Lost* and *Paradise Regained*—we have now learnt to enjoy them all and allow each man his own merits without complaining that he has not those of some one else. But there was some real sense and interest in the practice, if it could keep free from the Whig and Tory spirit that infected it too often. The use of the Opposition is to bring out the faults of the Ministry; they have nothing to do with its merits. But the literary critic is a judge whose summing up ought to give the strong points of both plaintiff and defendant. And when that is fairly done, or even honestly attempted, these literary parallels are not without their interest or their use. And in English literature there is not one more interesting than that between *Antony and Cleopatra* and *All for Love.*

The points of resemblance are, of course, obvious enough. The subject of both is the most famous of the world's love stories, and it is more than a mere community of subject, which has often existed between writers who never heard of each other. The principal source Dryden used in writing his play was not Plutarch or Appian or Dion Cassius; it was Shakespeare himself. 'In my style I have professed to imitate the divine Shakespeare'; and 'I hope I may affirm, and without vanity, that, by imitating him, I have excelled myself throughout the play.' So he tells us in his Preface, with noble modesty, in a day when men in general were still too near that mountain known as Shakespeare to realize its towering and unapproachable height. Yet the imitation is no slavish one. It owes much, but far from all, to its original. What did it receive and what does it bring? Well, there are some things that are receivable and some that are not. *Demens qui nimbos et non*

"Dryden and Shakespeare" by John Bailey. From The Times Literary Supplement, No. 116 *(April 1, 1904), p. 97ff. Reprinted by permission of* The Times Literary Supplement. *Abridged for this edition.*

imitabile fulmen, the eternal epitaph of those who do not know their place, would be the inevitable verdict on the fool who should try to retouch the unique incommunicable things of Shakespeare. No other man in the history of the world could quite have given us 'the baby at my breast, that sucks the nurse asleep'; other people who know their business will just let that alone for ever. And, though that stands by itself, the play has a good many other things of that high sort which meant death to the profane toucher. What is any other poet to do with 'Where's my serpent of old Nile?' or with the 'morsel cold upon dead Caesar's trencher,' or with 'O withered is the garland of the war,' or the passages of which they are merely the central jewels, except just to wonder and be silent? Who will need the warning voice to cry, 'touch not, taste not, handle not?'

Yet there is a good deal that Dryden found he could steal with honor and profit, and he has not feared to do so. But he has not forgotten that the poor are not entitled to more than the crumbs from the rich man's table. Many fragments will make one mouthful for him. Take such a passage as his

> There's no satiety of love in thee:
> Enjoyed, thou still art new: perpetual spring
> Is in thy arms: the ripened fruit but falls,
> And blossoms rise to fill its empty place:
> And I grow rich by giving.

It begins, of course, with a reminiscence of the incomparable 'Age cannot wither her, nor custom stale Her infinite variety'; but, as if to avoid direct rivalry with the magician, Dryden has transferred it to the mouth of Antony himself; and then it is mingled with gleanings from another great passage that Shakespeare had given to Cleopatra:

> For his bounty
> There was no winter in't: an autumn 'twas
> That grew the more by reaping:

and so the whole is put together and made the fine thing it is. Then, again, he could not pass over the great scene of Cleopatra in the barge. And he has borrowed well and wisely, taking what was in him to take, avoiding the Shakespearean conceits, and making a picture which is at once splendid and, even if avowedly after Shakespeare, still undoubtedly painted in his own manner. No one can do better such a thing as

> To soft flutes
> The silver oars kept time; and while they played,
> The hearing gave new pleasure to the sight;
> And both to thought.

But he dare not turn a bare word of Plutarch into such a picture as that of Antony alone in the deserted city 'enthroned i' the market-place' and 'whistling to the air'; and, if he is without Shakespeare's extravagances, he is equally without that lavish and royal exuberance which in Shakespeare makes every line ring with the reckless splendor of Cleopatra.

But if there is so much in Dryden that is borrowed, and so much more that it is his misfortune he could not borrow, how is it that *All for Love* is, after all, as some are bold enough to think, even more difficult to put down unfinished than *Antony and Cleopatra?* Broadly speaking, the answer is very simple. *Antony and Cleopatra* is drama in the shape of chronicle, *All for Love* is drama in the shape of drama. There is nothing Shakespeare could not do, when he chose; but even he, when he achieves the impossible, cannot get rid of all traces of the impossibility. And no occasional triumphs of genius will alter the fact that the drama is a confined form of literature and not an uncon-fined, that its field can never be all time, all place, and all existence, as that of the epic may almost be said to be, but that, other things being equal, it will succeed the better the closer it keeps to one time, one place, and one existence. There we get, of course, to the old battle of those famous unities, so long regarded in England as a mere piece of French pedantry. It is, no doubt, easy to exaggerate their importance; but it is easier still to exaggerate their unimportance. For see what they can do in such a case as the one before us. Nothing on earth, of course, could make Dryden Shakespeare's equal. But a small man working with the right tools will get nearer to a big man working with the wrong, than if both worked with the right or both with the wrong. These are relative words, of course, but one really need not go outside Shakespeare to see what a difference those derided unities, or rather the one important one, that of action or interest, can make. Why has *Othello* been thought by good judges to be the most moving play he wrote? Surely, not only for Desdemona's sake, but, if we think it out, because the action is more completely one than in any of the other tragedies. Why, again, do the great tragedies *Lear, Hamlet, Macbeth* take so much more complete possession of our whole being than the great Histories, *Julius Caesar,* or *Henry IV,* or this *Antony and Cleopatra?* For the same reason: that because these last are histories, they must be imperfect tragedies; for history and tragedy are not the same thing. No Falstaff or Brutus, or Cleopatra can quite compensate for that defect. For the drama has but a short time to do its work in, and to get it done the dramatist is wise to look neither to the right hand nor to the left, but to keep his eyes and ours fixed only on Hamlet's 'necessary question of the play.'

Many people, inclined to look on art and law as the enemies instead of the instruments of genius, will think this over-strict doctrine. To those who do may be commended the question, why Dryden in *All for Love* comes so much nearer Shakespeare than would naturally have been expected? Can they avoid the answer that it is not only that from his closeness to Shakespeare in this play he caught something of a spirit greater than his own, but also that he refused to load himself with encumbrances which make even Shakespeare's fiery energy reach the goal with difficulty, and would have prevented Dryden from reaching it at all? Who has not felt obliged in reading *Antony and Cleopatra* to turn back in bewilderment to the list of *dramatis personae*, as one unimportant personage after another fills the stage? Dryden is rid of that confusion at once: he has ten characters for Shakespeare's thirty-four. Then Shakespeare's action occupies twelve years, and takes place in about twelve different scenes; Dryden's all takes place at Alexandria, and in a few hours. But that is of less importance. The thing that makes the great difference is that *All for Love* is really what its name implies; whatever is said, done, or suffered, belongs to the love of Antony and to Cleopatra, and to nothing else at all. Here we have no Pompey or Lepidus, no rivalries of Triumvirs, no political intrigue, no superfluous or semi-superfluous scenes like some half-dozen or dozen of those in Shakespeare's play; here the circumference never forgets its center, 'every scene,' as Dryden says, 'conducing to the main design, and every Act concluding with a turn of it'; all moves forward steadily to the catastrophe, and we never for a moment lose sight of the immortal passion which is the whole of *All for Love,* the beginning and the middle and the end.

If we read the two plays with open minds, and are resolute to keep on this side idolatry in our thoughts of Shakespeare, it will surely be plain that in this matter of art and handling it is Dryden and not Shakespeare who has shown the sounder judgment. Shakespeare, in spite of his by-paths, may arrive first at the goal; but Dryden, by virtue of his straight road, is not so immeasurably far behind him. Nor is that his only virtue. Those who love fine things need not be afraid that *All for Love* will give them nothing but a well-designed general composition. It is full of glorious lines and brave sayings. Here, indeed, we must not think of Shakespeare; but, if we do not, will it not need some searching to find better things than Dolabella's

> Heaven has but
> Our sorrow for our sins.

or, in a very different vein, Antony's

> Let furies drag thee quick to hell; let all
> The longer damned have rest; each torturing hand
> Do thou employ, till Cleopatra comes.

or, again, Antony's grief—

> Then, art thou innocent, my poor dear love,
> And art thou dead?
> O those two words! their sound should be divided:
> Hadst thou been false, and died; or hadst thou lived,
> And hadst been true—But innocence and death!
> This shows not well above.

The thing in which Dryden hardly ever fails is his literary craftsmanship; but such things as these, and there are not a few of them, are enough to show that he had something in him which no mere art or training can ever give.

Cleopatra and "That Criticall Warr"

by Bonamy Dobrée

Since certain questions are no nearer solution than they were in the seventeenth century, it may not be altogether idle to try to analyze what actually happened with one subject when treated by poets whose methods differed.

The path it seems most useful to follow is one of inquiry into how much is gained or thrown away by writing within certain limits, and whether the profit outweighs the possible loss. If *Antony and Cleopatra* is better than *All for Love* is this due to advantages of method or of mind? And if to the latter, whether the genius of Shakespeare itself would not have benefited from the more austere discipline? for "great forces ask great labour in the management," as Davenant aptly pronounced. Our inquiry may also be aided by referring to Daniel's *Cleopatra,* which is composed on yet another method, being the extreme English example of the Senecan form, but which nevertheless throws light on certain aspects of the others. Unfortunately Sedley's play is too viciously bad to do more than serve as a source of interesting sidelights in the currents of contemporary thought and feeling as they affected Dryden.

All three poets worked on the same history, as translated by North, though Daniel may have gone to Plutarch or Amyot, and it is supposed that he studied Garnier's *Marc-Antoine;* but the arrangement of the incidents of the story is in each case different. Daniel's theme is the sorrow of a woman who *has been* Cleopatra and who, bereft of Antony, struggles between, on the one hand her desire to obtain a heritage for her children, and on the other her horror of making a Roman holiday. She ultimately finds a refuge in death. His theme is narrowed to the utmost limit. Dryden's is the struggle between Cleopatra and the Egyptians on one side, Ventidius and Rome on the other, for Antony himself, which ends through the natural turns of

"Cleopatra and 'That Criticall Warr'" by Bonamy Dobrée. From The Times Literary Supplement, No. 1393 *(October 11, 1928), pp. 717-18. Copyright 1928 by* The Times Literary Supplement. *Reprinted by permission of* The Times Literary Supplement *and the author. Slightly abridged for this edition.*

passion in the death of the lovers. Shakespeare's is difficult to disentangle, being of too wide a sweep for definition. Perhaps it would be safest to say that his is merely the general tragic theme, illustrating the sort of thing which happens to mankind; but if we try to describe it we may say it combines those of Daniel and Dryden, and adds to them a vast theme of empire. It is stretched to the farthest limit. There is, in short, no main theme to take hold of.

We may now plunge into "that Criticall warr which never ceases amongst the learned," and ask how far Shakespeare was hampered by what we may call the "panoramic" method. One disadvantage of this method is at once clear; alone, it no more clarifies the emotions than the raw life. To make a tragedy out of North's history, we have ourselves to do the work of the tragedian; but the business of a playwright is not to give us the materials for a tragedy, but by the especial ordering of the materials to compel a peculiar balance. The amount of obstructive material in *Antony and Cleopatra* is in consequence enormous. In construction alone—to leave out such considerations we are offered as to whether a eunuch has passions, or such additions as the "ragging" of Lepidus on Pompey's ship—one need but point to the Actium scenes, or to that of Ventidius in Syria. The play is full of events which are not action. And here the question may pertinently be put: What do the first three acts of *Antony and Cleopatra* actually do towards ordering our emotions? This may perhaps best be answered by suggesting that it would not be at all incongruous for the play to end as a comedy, a result unthinkable at that stage in the plays of either Daniel or Dryden. If these acts are unnecessary to the tragedy, they are obstructive, for time also is an important factor, since the tragic balance is not to be compelled all at once. Shakespeare was forced to contract all the tragic elements into the last two acts; and even the final speech of the play is marred because he still had something to tell us which he found in North—namely, that Cleopatra had experimented in poisons.

The alternative to panoramic history is "relation," the telling of the tale, which has the disadvantage that it hangs up the action, a problem Ibsen was the first to solve. We suspend the flow of our emotions to consider history. There is, for instance, a dangerous moment in Act I of *The Tempest,* and in actual performance it is not always Miranda alone who is "inclined to sleep." But relation has this advantage: it allows of the full development of thought and comment. It involves, however, a much lower key if it is to be maintained, with the result that Daniel's play, which is almost entirely in relation (owing to his predilection for a certain form which was not thrust upon him), gives us "rather a beautiful statue than a breather." Nevertheless, relation has its place, and can be extremely effective in short passages, espe-

cially if it bears not on the event of the moment but upon its emotions, for the past is only important as it affects the present.

> He at Philippi kept
> His sword, e'en like a dancer; while I struck
> The lean and wrinkled Cassius.

This, Hazlitt says, "is one of those fine retrospections which shows us
the winding and eventful march of human life." Yet Dryden, working
within the unities, can do precisely the same as Shakespeare, and on
a larger scale than that of the passage Hazlitt quoted:—

> How I lov'd
> Witness ye days and nights, and all ye hours
> That danc'd away with down upon your feet,
> As all your business were to count my passion.
> One day past by, and nothing saw but love;
> Another came, and still 'twas only love.

This advantage, then, of the panoramic method seems to be without
foundation; for what of retrospective do the first three acts of *Antony
and Cleopatra* do that *All for Love* does not?

If it be right to assume that the effect of a drama is attained by
movement of the emotions, it would appear that the panoramic method
has one enormous advantage over the classical, for with each different
scene—and there are thirty-eight in *Antony and Cleopatra*—a change
in speed can at once be brought about. This is of prime value, and
it might be possible to judge a play by its rhythmic structure alone.
Yet to read *All for Love* immediately after *Antony and Cleopatra* is
seriously to undermine one's opinion of the gain. For by Shakespeare's
method there is room for only one emotion in each scene: the play
proceeds by violent contrasts; the swaying back and forth of the emotions which will eventually lead to the "full repose" (the term is
Dryden's) is spasmodic. Shakespeare has to show Antony in a rage,
or wild with jealousy, except when he speaks coldly, politically, and
with thought which is not action, since it does nothing to develop
character. His mind does not unfold itself as it does in *All for Love:*
it is shown in a series of sharp disjuncted images, and therefore remains crude. On the other side, the keeping of each act entire allows
for development of character and a much subtler, surer, emotive
progression. But of these things it is almost impossible to speak, because to substantiate the argument would need the quotation of a
whole act from each play. Each act of *All for Love,* as Dryden claimed,
concludes with a turn of the main design, not only of action, but of
the emotion, that leads to the action which is to complete it. Of the

kind of thing here meant the first scene between Antony and Cleopatra
may be noted, though the illustration must be imperfect since it is
fragmentary. Antony, having been won over by Ventidius, is being
drawn back by Cleopatra, who is speaking:—

> How shall I plead my cause, when you, my judge,
> Already have condemned me? Shall I bring
> The love you bore me for my advocate?
> That now is turned against me, that destroys me?
> For love, once past, is, at the best, forgotten;
> But oftener sours to hate: 'twill please my Lord
> To ruin me, and therefore I'll be guilty.
> But, could I once have thought it would have pleased you
> That you would pry, with narrow, searching eyes
> Into my faults, severe to my destruction,
> And watching all advantages with care,
> That serve to make me wretched? Speak, my lord,
> For I end here. Though I deserved this usage,
> Was it like you to give it?

It may with justice be argued that all this is too lifelike; that
Shakespeare, with his intensification of reality, takes us out of the
bounds of realism; that he has created a world which is not life, but
like it; and that unless we accept his premises we have not the right
of entry into his realm. This is cogent; it is, indeed, the answer to
Rymer on *Othello;* but for it to be valid the play needs to have a
complete consistency, a rigorous exclusion of naturalism which Shakespeare did not achieve; nor could he, if he were to give nearly every
"event" mentioned by North. One has only to point to the scenes
where Cleopatra receives the news of Antony's marriage to Octavia
(ii. 5 and iii. 3) to illustrate the occasional lapse into complete realism.
Shakespeare perhaps tried to avoid this, for often one feels that he is
forcing the note to something beyond the natural; and this suggests
another serious disadvantage in his method, which is that to keep the
drama interesting the historical and merely "eventful" part has to be
heightened, so that the main actors in the drama seem to be in a
passion equally high over indifferent things as over the significant
actions. Take the first lines Antony and Cleopatra speak, not, it is true,
over an indifferent thing, but at an insignificant moment:—

> *Cleopatra.* If it be love indeed, tell me how much.
> *Antony.* There's beggary in the love that can be reckoned.
> *Cleopatra.* I'll set a bourn how far to be beloved.
> *Antony.* Then must thou needs find out new heav'n, new earth.

At this point it is that one of the more important questions must be asked, which is, How far does form affect the diction and phrasing? and whether in this sphere the greater liberty of the panoramic form may not make up for its disadvantages? It would appear that form and phrasing are inextricably dependent upon one another. However, it is curious to note how Shakespeare is always "classical" in the vivid imagery of his metaphor, whereas Daniel, with his vague suggestiveness, is much more "romantic"—*e.g.*, "When that inexorable monster death," or purely intellectual, as in "those summer swallows of felicity." Perhaps, indeed probably, no rigid dividing line can be drawn between what is possible or impossible within the various forms, and the most that one can say is that one form favors one diction rather than another; at all events, in these three plays there are certain facts to be reckoned and certain comparisons to be made.

Daniel's play is written in quatrains, but the occasional couplets often give the effect of complete sonnets in the Shakespearian manner. Dryden's is written in blank verse, "in imitation of the divine Shakespeare," but it is a verse very much less flexible than his original's; for in truth Dryden was incapable of that great and subtle variety of rhythm, of all those undertones and modulations which are the gift of Shakespeare alone. We must try to distinguish what is due to form, and what to difference in genius. But since in the classical way of writing it is essential to preserve a unity of tone, not a uniformity, but a change within definite limits, it would appear that to sustain this the poet must deny himself certain peaks, and, if not the more deeply searching phrases, the livelier extraneous pictures. He must certainly adjure the wilder flights of rhetoric. Shakespeare can afford to be splendidly rhetorical.

> Dissolve thick clouds and rain, that I may say
> The gods themselves do weep,

comes perfectly in *Antony and Cleopatra*, but would appear forced in *All for Love*. In the classical method all must be borne outward on an irresistible tide. Not that all Shakespeare's finest flashes would be inappropriate. The superb

> Peace! Peace!
> Dost thou see my baby at my breast
> That sucks the nurse asleep?

might well have a place in *All for Love*, had not Dryden studiously avoided taking anything of importance from Shakespeare. Certainly if you can say with Dryden

> When half the world fell mould'ring from my hands,

you must admit Shakespeare's

> Finish good lady; the bright day is done,
> And we are for the dark.

But the question arises, though you can say

> What to be led in triumph through the streets,
> A spectacle to base Plebeian eyes;
> Whilst some dejected friend of Antony's
> Close in a corner, shakes his head and mutters
> A secret curse on her who ruined him.

is it possible to be as graphic as

> saucy lictors
> Will catch at us like strumpets; and scald rhymers
> Ballad us out o' tune: the quick comedians
> Extemporally will stage us, and present
> Our Alexandrian revels. Antony
> Shall be brought drunken forth, and I shall see
> Some squeaking Cleopatra boy my greatness
> I' the posture of a whore.

Is that compatible with the classical form?

Let us now take a passage which shows the variance in diction of the three methods, from which it would appear that the formal method of relation slows down too much, but that the panoramic method, with its naturalism forced to rhetorical heights, brings about a diffusion. The scene is described in North:—

> But when they had opened the doors they found Cleopatra stark dead, laid upon a bed of gold, attired and arrayed in her royal robes and one of her two women, which was called Iras, dead at her feet: and her other woman called Charmion half-dead, and trembling, trimming the diadem which Cleopatra wore upon her head. One of the soldiers seeing her, angrily said unto her: "Is that well done, Charmion?" "Very well", said she again, "and meet for a princess descended from the race of so many noble kings". She said no more, but fell down dead hard by the bed.

Daniel:—

> For there they found stretcht on a bed of gold.
> Dead Cleopatra; and that proudly dead,
> In all the rich attire procure she could;
> And dying Charmian trimming of her head.
> And Eras at her feet, dead in like case.

> Charmian, is this well done? said one of them.
> Yea, well said she, and her that from the race
> Of so great kings descends, doth best become,
> And with that word, yields to her faithful breath,
> To pass th' assurance of her love with death.

Shakespeare:—

[Eros had died after kissing Cleopatra, which elicits the terrible "Have I the aspic in my lips?" When Cleopatra dies Charmian says:]

> So, fare thee well.
> Now boast thee death, in thy possession lies
> A lass unparallel'd. Downy windows, close;
> And golden Phoebus never be beheld
> Of eyes again so royal! Your crown's awry;
> I'll mend it, and then play.
>
> *(Enter Guards, rushing in.)*

First Guard.	Where is the queen?
Charmian.	Speak softly, wake her not.
First Guard.	Caesar hath sent—
Charmian.	Too slow a messenger.

> *(Applies the asp.)*
> O! Come; apace; despatch: I partly feel thee.

First Guard.	Approach, ho! All's not well: Caesar's beguiled.
Second Guard.	There's Dolabella sent from Caesar; call him.
First Guard.	What work is here?—Charmian, is this well done?
Charmion.	It is well done, and fitting for a princess

> Descended of so many royal kings.
> Ah, soldier!
>
> *(Dies)*

Dryden:—

[Cleopatra and Iras are dead; Antony dead beside Cleopatra.] *Charmion stands behind her chair as dressing her head. Enter Serapion, two priests, Alexas bound, Egyptians.*

Second Priest.	Behold, Serapion, what havoc death has made.
Serapion.	'Twas what I fear'd—Charmion, is this well done?
Charmion.	Yes, 'tis well done, and like a Queen, the last

> Of her great race, I follow her.
>
> *(Sinks down and dies.)*

In Charmian's last speech it would seem that Dryden has the advantage, simply because of the more measured and restrained flow of his verse. Yet the passage from Daniel serves to show the advantage of

relation, for the spoken word is often more impressive than the thing
enacted before us. The beautiful line

> And dying Charmian trimming of her head

is merely a stage direction in Dryden. Shakespeare, feeling the need
to supplement the action by words, put in "Your crown's awry, I'll
mend it, and then play"; but powerful as those plain words are after
the flowery passage, it is doubtful if they are as moving as Daniel's.

In his "Defence of Rhyme" Daniel remarked of it that "in an emi-
nent spirit, whom nature hath fitted for that mystery, rhyme is no
impediment to his conceit, but rather gives him wings to mount, and
carries him, not out of his course, but as it were beyond his power
to farre happier flight," a conclusion M. Paul Valéry has also reached:
"Elle y appelle de très loin une multitude de pensées qui ne s'attendait
pas d'être conçues." Certainly, for its effect on the listener, in ordering the impulses to one end, it is very valuable; but it may be doubted
if Daniel's argument is applicable to the stage, the more so when we
remember that Dryden's argument was the exact reverse. "The benefit
I consider most in it," he wrote in his Epistle Dedicatory of *The Rival
Ladies*, "is that it bounds and circumscribes the fancy. For imagination in a poet is a faculty so wild and lawless, that like an high-
ranging spaniel, it must have clogs tied to it lest it outrun the judgment." But he was speaking of the couplet, which as he used it does
indeed have the effect he states; for even in *Aureng-Zebe*, his freest
attempt, the grammatical unit seldom overflows the couplet. But
though abandoning rhyme for this play, he tightened up blank verse,
which had so much run to seed in Shakespeare's successors. In so
doing he definitely denied himself the broader rhythm, the wider
sweep; but Daniel, in using the quatrain, surely gave himself too
large a unit, which too much slows down and distends the thought:—

> When yet we reckon life our dearest good,
> And so we live, we care not how we live!
> So deep we feel impressed in our blood
> That touch which nature without breath did give—
> And yet what blasts of words hath Learning found
> To blow against the fear of death and dying,

and he takes eighteen more lines to exhaust the idea. Dryden is pithy,
and accomplishes in four lines the same thing it took Daniel twenty
to do:—

> O that I less could fear to lose this being,
> Which, like a snowball in my coward hand,
> The more 'tis grasped, the faster melts away.

> Poor reason, what a wretched aid art thou!
> For still, in spite of thee,
> These two long lovers, soul and body, dread
> Their final separation.

Whatever the demerits of the couplet may be, it is evidently splendid training.

But if Dryden is magnificently condensed, the advantage is not always with the more restrained form; and here is an example where the naturalistic method seems to gain over the others. The idea is not in North; but it is in Daniel, where Nuntius relates:—

> Well, in I went, where brighter than the sunne
> Glittering in all her pompeous rich array
> Great Cleopatra sat, as if sh' had won
> Caesar, and all the world beside, this day:
> Even as she was when on thy crystal streams
> Cleare Cydnos, she did show what earth could show;
> When Asia all amazed in wonder deemes
> Venus from heaven was come on earth below.
> Even as she went at first to meet her love
> So goes she now again to find him.
> But that first did her greatness only prove,
> This last her love, that could not live behind him.

Dryden, in strict conformity with the tone of the whole act, has:—

Charmion.	To what end
	These ensigns of your pomp and royalty?
Cleopatra.	Dull that thou art! why 'tis to meet my love;
	As when I saw him first on Cydnos bank
	All sparkling, like a goddess; so adorned
	I'll find him once again. My second spousals
	Shall match my first in glory. Haste, haste, both,
	And dress the bride of Antony.

But this is Shakespeare:—

> Show me, my women, like a queen: go fetch
> My best attires; I am again for Cydnus
> To meet Mark Antony.

There is no doubt there which is the most dramatic and pithy, and therefore the most poetic.

Shakespeare's fancy is not one to wish bounded and circumscribed, though, we are sometimes glad, in Dryden, to be rid of the earlier euphuism and references to pagan gods. Nevertheless Shakespeare's

verse sometimes ran away with him: the following passage is magnificent, but would it not be better without the last line, which is
something of an example of sinking?

> For his bounty
> There was no winter in't; an autumn 'twas
> That grew the more by reaping: his delights
> Were Dolphin-like; they showed his back above
> The element they liv'd in: in his livery
> Walk'd crowns and crownets; realms and islands were
> As plates dropped from his pocket.

The whole speech, with its beginning "His legs bestrid the Ocean,"
is a superb piece of rhetoric, far outdistancing Dryden's

> We two have kept its homage in suspense,
> And bent the globe on whose each side we trod
> Till it was dented inwards,

fine as it is, and the parallel passage in Shakespeare is, "We could not
stall together in the whole world." Whether a stricter manner of writing would have caused Shakespeare to have blotted his last line is
doubtful, but it would certainly have prevented him from writing
such a line as

> And foist him up to the shouting plebeians.

But if the classical method may save from false, it prevents the rise
to the heights of right rhetoric, that summit of the dramatist's art;
and Dryden, where he makes Antony compare himself with Mars, is
perilously near bombast. Yet he can rise very high:—

> O horror, horror!
> Egypt has been: our latest hour is come:
> The Queen of Nations from her ancient seat
> Is sunk for ever in the dark abyss:
> Time has unrolled her glories to the last
> And now clos'd up the volume.

Yet it seems to lack the larger rhythm; the influence of the couplet is
here too circumscribing; apart from the question of actual thought,
the manner would hardly admit

> O! see my women,
> The crown o' the earth doth melt. My lord!
> O! withered is the garland of the war,
> The soldier's pole is fallen: young boys and girls
> Are level now with men: the odds is gone,

> And there is nothing left remarkable
> Beneath the visiting moon.

It is, perhaps, not altogether fair to divorce a passage from its context, for the setting counts for much, and this consideration must modify any conclusion to be drawn from parallels. Almost the same words may have quite a different effect when variously placed; how much so may be seen from a phrase of Shakespeare's Antony already quoted here, and one of Claudio's in *Measure for Measure*

> I will encounter darkness as a bride
> And hug it in my arms.

Remy de Gourmont remarked that "Un livre que la vénération des siècles a sacré n'est plus un livre; c'est une partie de la nature"—that is, it is extremely hard to separate it from our associations. But if the effect of tragedy is, after adventuring to produce free contemplation, detached from personal fears and desires, disilluded, it is clear from nearly all the critics who have written of it that Shakespeare's play fails of this effect. There is hardly one who has not been left in love with Cleopatra, feeling that life is rich and exciting, who is not, in sum, swayed by the emotions a gorgeous story provokes. The proof that they are beglamoured lies in their very panegyrics upon Cleopatra. Grave and reverend signors declare her to be the flower of womanhood, the *ewige weibliche,* as Leda, the mother of Helen of Troy, as St. Anne, the mother of Mary. This is a strange conception, due, perhaps to that very English desire, the other side of the Puritan medal, to find a woman to whom they could physically and morally abandon themselves, though in reality they might flee from her arms to those of the mother of the Gracchi. For turn what Shakespeare says into the prose of the daily paper, see the object as it really is, and she appears as vulgar as Plutarch makes her, fit indeed for a gaudy night, but preposterous, superficial, cruel, greedy, of the flesh, fleshy, with intelligence only enough to make a pun upon the name Toryne, to practice the seductive arts of a low-born trollop, and cause salted fish to be placed upon Antony's hook—treatment, by the way, he richly deserved. Not a man of these critics but would be Antony if he could; but who would be Œdipus, Phèdre, or Lear?

It may be said that all the foregoing observations are beside the point, since the object of Shakespeare was not that of Daniel or of Dryden. These last were definitely aiming at the production of a certain effect by carefully selecting their elements, and expressing them in an especial economy. Dryden, to set aside Daniel's less dramatic poem, undoubtedly achieves a great and sustained beauty. He had, to use an expression of Landor's, this of godlike in him, a love of order

and the power of bringing great things into it. Shakespeare seems to
be aiming at something which comes from below the sense of, or the
desire for, beauty; his work is informed by a more inclusive feeling.
After reading *All for Love* we are conscious of having heard glorious
music; after reading *Antony and Cleopatra* the voices of men and
women, the clash of events, resound in our ears, and the music is but
an incidental, if prevailing, element.

But to whatever extent doubt may overcast the possible conclusions
here suggested, one thing is certain, the classical method rigorously
excludes comic relief. Not necessarily humour, as Ventidius's apt and
admirable speech to Alexas is enough to show:—

> There's news for you; run, my officious eunuch,
> Be sure to be the first; haste forward.
> Haste, my dear eunuch, haste.

Yet it definitely cuts out that use of the comic to throw into high light
the agony of terrible events, a relief Shakespeare used to the full in the
scene where the "clown" brings Cleopatra the asps. The danger of such
relief is that it may harrow too much, that the subtle structure of
appetencies and satisfactions may be deranged. Our emotions may be
disordered so as to seek relief, in the other sense of the word, by
hysterical laughter or a sob; and this is not the end of tragedy. The
clown scene is indeed strong meat to digest, into any ordered system,
and it is questionable whether the general tone of Shakespeare's play
will bear it, as *Lear* bears similar scenes. It would certainly destroy
All for Love. Yet such contrasts, if successful, probe more deeply than
anything common in the classical method. Think, in Shakespeare, of
Antony's twice repeated "I'm dying, Egypt, dying," flung against Cleopatra's wild, egotistical almost "low" babble. The phrase comes with
terrible effect; it is a tremendous summation; but its simplicity, its
grandeur, would be lost in the general grandeur of *All for Love.* It
would come greatly anywhere, but not with that supreme force with
which Shakespeare invests it.

In the main, it is Shakespeare's poetic genius in the use of metaphor,
his incomparable capacity for marrying ideas, his irresistible mind
working ever on the word and making it flesh, which makes his play
more universal than Dryden's. It is chokefull of unforgettable things;
the play would furnish forth half a dozen of *All for Love,* good poet
though Dryden be. Dryden in the use of the lambent phrase, the
metaphor that vanquishes or seduces, in the revealing word that
lightens like a flash, is far below Shakespeare, Webster or Tourneur.

Yet, in its result, *All for Love* is more decisively a tragedy than any
of those above referred to except Shakespeare's best, and *Antony and*

Cleopatra is not one of them. Many other plays contain finer things than Dryden ever wrote, but as wholes they are patchy. Their makers were never certain within what limits they worked; or they defiantly flouted the limits, like Webster, who declared, "Willingly, and not ignorantly, in this kind have I faulted." Thus their works are not in their final effect so near tragedy as Dryden's masterpiece. The barriers of form justify themselves in actual practice, for the frame of the panoramic play is too diffuse; it contains too many emotional values, in number beyond the power of ordering. Dryden's play has a coherence, a direction to one end, in a word, a unity which we may wrest from the others, but which they do not, like his, compel.

The Imagery of *All for Love*

by *Kenneth Muir*

All for Love was avowedly written in imitation of Shakespeare's style, though, as Professor Dobrée observes, "Dryden was not trying to do at all the same kind of thing as Shakespeare." A comparison of the play with *Antony and Cleopatra* is a favorite theme of critics. On the one hand Professor Dobrée claims that Dryden's play "has a more tragic effect"; while, on the other hand, Mr. Leavis has little difficulty in showing the superiority of Shakespeare's description of the Cydnus episode to that of his imitator.

It is now generally agreed that Shakespeare's supereminence as a poetic dramatist depends to a considerable extent on the power of his imagery, and the measure of Dryden's inferiority cannot better be shown than by an examination of the play in which he came nearest to Shakespeare. The following brief observations in no way conflict with Mr. Jefferson's interesting essay on Dryden's Heroic Plays.

There are rather more than two hundred images in *All for Love* but there is no evidence that Dryden employs what Miss Spurgeon calls "iterative imagery." Many of his images fall naturally into groups, but there is no outstanding one as in many of Shakespeare's plays. It must be admitted that there is one group consisting of 20 images drawn from astronomy and cosmology; but in this Dryden was merely imitating Shakespeare. As Miss Spurgeon has shown, the dominating image-group in *Antony and Cleopatra* is precisely this. The other considerable groups may be tabulated as follows—

Wild Beasts	10
Sea, etc.	10
Drugs, etc.	10
War	8
Law	7
Astrology	7

"The Imagery of All for Love*" by Kenneth Muir. From* Proceedings of the Leeds Philosophical and Literary Society, *V (1940), pp. 140-47. Copyright 1940 by The Leeds Philosophical and Literary Society and the author. Reprinted by permission of the Leeds Philosophical and Literary Society and the author.*

Storms, etc.   6
Shipwreck   5

Unfortunately Miss Spurgeon's method of classification has the disadvantage of ranking together images which are striking and original
with those which have become staled through much repetition; and it
must be confessed that the great majority of Dryden's images are extremely conventional. In fact, in a large number of cases, the images
are at best in a state of suspended animation. It will give a far clearer
idea of the imagery of the play, if, instead of considering all the 200
images, we eliminate such commonplace poeticisms as the following—

A foolish Dream,
Bred from the fumes of indigested Feasts . . .
Yet still War seems on either side to sleep . . .
. . . makes his Heart a Prey to black despair . . .
This changes my designs, this blasts my Counsels . . .
. . . this is no common Dew.

These five examples are all taken from the first few pages of the
play. Nothing can be learned from them about Dryden's conscious or
unconscious conception of his subject; and if such images are left out
of consideration, there remain less than 50 significant images. In other
words, less than a quarter of Dryden's images have any poetical significance. The proportion with Shakespeare is, of course, much higher.
Even some of the remaining 40 or 50 images are seriously defective.
Ventidius' remark about Antony in Act I—

Virtue's his path; but sometimes 'tis too narrow
For his vast Soul . . .

is morally and poetically unsound. In the same act, his praise of
Antony sounds like flattery, though it is vitally important that it should
seem sincere—

the Gods who form'd you, wonder'd
At their own skill, and cry'd, A lucky hit
Has mended our design . . .

and in the third act, in Antony's description of his friendship with
Dolabella, Dryden as well as Antony is too obviously searching for
suitable comparisons—

I was his Soul; he liv'd not but in me:
We were so clos'd within each others Breasts,
The Rivets were not found that join'd us first.
That does not reach us yet: we were so mixt,

> As meeting Streams, both to our selves were lost;
> We were one Mass; we could not give or take,
> But from the same . . .

In the fourth act, Dolabella's account of Antony's desertion of Cleopatra contains the invalid comparison—

> What endless Treasure hast thou thrown away,
> And scatter'd, like an Infant, in the Ocean,
> Vain sums of Wealth which none can gather thence.

How inadequate this image is may best be seen putting beside it Othello's famous words—

> of one whose hand,
> Like the base *Indian*, threw a pearle away,
> Richer then all his Tribe . . .

Even more absurd are Antony's lines addressed to Dolabella and Cleopatra—

> how could you betray
> This tender Heart, which with an Infant-fondness
> Lay lull'd betwixt your Bosoms, and there slept
> Secure of injur'd Faith?

The unforunate baby is precariously perched between two different bosoms (Cleopatra's and Dolabella's); and apart from the practical difficulties, there seems to be no special appropriateness in the image. A heart cannot be compared to a baby without absurdity; and Antony was hardly as inexperienced as the comparison would imply.

One other example of false imagery may be given. It occurs in the last speech of the play, where Serapion addresses the dead lovers—

> Sleep, blest Pair,
> Secure from humane Chance, long Ages out,
> While all the Storms of Fate fly o'er your Tomb . . .

The word "fly" betrays the falsity of Dryden's imagination.

It would be wrong to imply that Dryden is usually guilty of such imagery. Many of his images are entirely satisfying. Our conception of Antony is enlarged by the lines—

> fortune striding, like a vast *Colossus*,
> Cou'd fix an equal foot of Empire here . . .

though they are clearly based on a well-known passage in *Julius Caesar*. Antony's state is well described in the lines of Ventidius—

> Shrunk from the vast extent of all his Honours,
> And crampt within a corner of the World . . .

and Antony's lines about Octavius are even more impressive—

> drives me before him,
> To the World's ridge, and sweeps me off like rubbish.

In the same way a number of images really illuminate Dryden's conception of Cleopatra. She declares that she has soared "quite out of Reason's view." Alexas tells her that love deludes her sight.

> As, what is strait, seems crooked through the Water . . .

Dolabella compares her to "a Rock of solid Chrystal"; and Alexas declares that—

> at her Feet were laid
> The Scepters of the Earth, expos'd on heaps,
> To choose where she would Reign.

Antony's self-knowledge could not be better expressed than in the vivid image—

> I am made a shallow-forded Stream,
> Seen to the bottom . . .

and in two images of almost Shakespearean intensity, Antony conveys the grandeur and the tragedy of his love—

> While within your Arms I lay,
> The World fell mouldring from my Hands each Hour,
> And left me scarce a grasp . . .

> 'Tis time the World
> Shou'd have a Lord, and know whom to obey.
> We two have kept its Homage in suspence,
> And bent the Globe on whose each side we trod,
> Till it was dinted inwards . . .

The last group of images to be discussed is the most important and the most typically Dryden's. It consists of long similes, twelve in number, and those who profess great admiration for Dryden's blank verse invariably quote one or more of these twelve.

In one or two of these similes, the comparison is pressed to the borders of the ludicrous—

> Thou find'st me at my lowest Water-mark,
> The Rivers that ran in, and rais'd my Fortunes,

> Are all dry'd up, or take another course:
> What I have left is from my native Spring;
> I've still a Heart that swells, in scorn of Fate,
> And lifts me to my Banks.

The words of the dying Antony have perhaps lost some of their dignity through the debasing of the word *remove;* but they can never have struck a note perfectly in harmony with the rest of the scene—

> 'Tis as with a Man
> Removing in a hurry; all pack'd up,
> But one dear Jewel that his haste forgot;
> And he, for that returns upon the spur:
> So I come back, for thee.

The remaining images in this group are extremely effective, and they contain some of Dryden's best poetry. A few of them are well known—the passage in the first act beginning—

> How I lov'd
> Witness ye Days and Nights, and all your Hours . . .

and Dolabella's speech in Act IV,

> Men are but Children of a larger growth . . .

which, apart from its lack of rhyme, recalls the best passages of the heroic plays, represent the summit of Dryden's achievement in dramatic poetry. But there are others as fine, of which one example must suffice—

> Does the mute Sacrifice upbraid the Priest?
> He knows him not his Executioner.
> O, she has deck'd his ruin with her Love,
> Led him in Golden Bands to gaudy slaughter,
> And made perdition pleasing.[1]

The general debt of Dryden to Shakespeare was acknowledged in the preface to *All for Love.* He mentions particularly the first scene between Antony and Ventidius, as being superior to anything he had written "in this kind." He might have added that the character of Ventidius is clearly modelled on that of Enobarbus, and that the scene itself owes a little to the quarrel scene in *Julius Caesar.* In certain set speeches, such as the description of the Barge on the Cydnus, Dryden is following Shakespeare as well as Plutarch. These facts are well known; but, so far as I know, there has been no satisfactory account

---

[1] See also I, 337-49; III, 212-17; IV, 92-6, 236-41; V, 35-49, 388-91.

of Dryden's borrowings of Shakespearean imagery. More than 20 of
the images of the play—i.e. 10 per cent—are directly borrowed or imitated from Shakespeare; and 13 of these are, as we might expect, taken
from *Antony and Cleopatra*. A few examples will indicate the nature
of the debt—

> *Caesar* stept in, and with a greedy hand
> Pluck'd the green Fruit . . .
> > (*A.L.* II.311-2)

> My Sallad dayes,
> When I was greene in judgement . . .
> > (*A.C.* I.v.73-4)

> loos'nd Nature
> Leap from its hinges. Sink the props of Heav'n,
> And fall the Skies to crush the neather World.
> > (*A.L.* II.489-91)

> Let Rome in Tyber melt, and the wide Arch
> Of the raing'd Empire fall . . .
> > (*A.C.* I,i.33-34)

> Age buds at sight of her, and swells to youth:
> The holy Priests gaze on her when she smiles;
> And with heav'd hands forgetting Gravity,
> They bless her wanton Eyes . . .
> > (*A.L.* IV.272-5)

> For vildest things
> Become themselves in her, that the holy Priests
> Blesse her, when she is Riggish.
> > (*A.C.* II.ii.243-5)

> Let *Cæsar* take the World,—
> An empty Circle, since the Jewel's gone
> Which made it worth my strife . . .
> > (*A.L.* V.310-2)

> this World did equall theyrs,
> Till they had stolne our Iewell.
> > (*A.C.* IV.xv.77-8)

> While hand in hand we walk in Groves below,
> Whole Troops of Lovers Ghosts shall flock about us,
> And all the Train be ours.
> > (*A.L.* V.455-8)

> Where Soules do couch on Flowers, we'll hand in hand,
> And with our sprightly Port make the Ghostes gaze:
> *Dido,* and her *Æneas* shall want Troopes,
> And all the haunt be ours.
>
> (*A.C.* IV.xiv.52-5)

> his Wife, my *Charmion;*
> For 'tis to that high Title I aspire . . .
>
> (*A.L.* V.475-6)

> Husband, I come:
> Now to that name, my Courage proue my Title.
>
> (*A.C.* V.ii.290-1)

> Only thou
> Cou'dst triumph o'er thy self; and thou alone
> Wert worthy so to triumph.
>
> (*A.L.* V.522-4)

> *Anthonie's* hath Triumpht on it selfe . . .
> A Roman, by a Roman
> Valiantly vanquish'd.
>
> (*A.C.* IV.xv.15, 57-8)

> And thinks himself but Sleep . . .
> Y'are in the Toils . . .
> Th' inevitable Charms, that catch
> Mankind so sure . . .
> he's not the first
> For whom you spread your snares . . .
>
> (*A.L.* V.550, II.261, III.499-500, 489-90)

> she lookes like sleepe,
> As she would catch another *Anthony*
> In her strong toyle of Grace.
>
> (*A.C.* V.ii.349-351)

Dryden was indebted not only to Shakespeare. The last act of *All for Love* is both the richest in imagery and the finest from the dramatic point of view. Five of the images in this act are, as we have seen, imitated from Shakespeare; and Dryden's imitations are naturally inferior to the originals. It has not yet been pointed out how many of the remaining images in this act Dryden owed to Samuel Daniel, whose tragedy, *Cleopatra,* in the Senecan style, deals with the events after the death of Antony. Professor Dobrée's essay comparing the three plays, though it gives high praise to Daniel, does not raise the question of Dryden's borrowings. Yet they were considerable, and unacknowledged. It is not too much to say that the effectiveness of Act V depends very largely on echoes from Daniel's play.[2]

Most of the passages imitated by Dryden occur in the last act of Daniel's play and in the last 150 lines of *All for Love*. A few come earlier. Daniel's Cleopatra, referring to the desertion of her followers, remarks—

> Witnesse these gallant fortune-following traines,
> These Summer Swallowes of felicity
> Gone with the heate: of all, see what remaines,
> This monument, two maydes, and wretched I.

Dryden puts the same idea into the mouth of Antony to describe the defection of Cleopatra—

> Ingrateful Woman!
> Who follow'd me, but as the Swallow Summer, . . .
> But, now my Winter comes, she spreads her wings,
> And seeks the Spring of *Cæsar*

Cleopatra, in Daniel's play, says she is

> Reseru'd for bands to grace proud *Cæsars* state
> Who seeks in me to triumph ouer thee

Dryden echoes the last line—

> *Cæsar* shall triumph o'er no part of thee.

The remaining echoes occur after Antony's death. Daniel's Cleopatra cries—

> 'Tis sweet to die when we are forced to liue . . .

and her words are echoed by Dryden's—

> 'Tis sweet to die, when they wou'd force life on me.

Daniel, in describing the way Cleopatra adorns herself for death, uses the following words—

> Euen as she was when on thy christall streames,
> Cleare *Cydnos*, she did shew what earth could shew;
> When *Asia* all amaz'd in wonder, seemes
> Venus from heauen was come on earth below.
> Euen as she went at first to meete her loue . . .

---

[2] This paragraph was published before I had seen Summers' edition of Dryden's plays in which many of the parallels with Daniel are quoted.

Dryden's Cleopatra is quite clearly echoing them in the following speech—

> why, 'tis to meet my love;
> As when I saw him first, on *Cydnos* bank,
> All sparkling, like a Goddess.

In the fourth act of Daniel's play, Cleopatra addresses the tomb of Antony—

> And you deare reliques of my Lord and Loue,
> (The sweetest parcels of the faithfull'st liuer,)
> O let no impious hand dare to remoue
> You out from hence, but rest you here for euer.
> Let *Egypt* now giue peace vnto you dead,
> That liuing, gaue you trouble and turmoile.

Cleopatra in *All for Love*, left alone with the body of Antony, uses almost identical words—

> Hail, you dear Relicks
> Of my Immortal Love!
> O let no Impious hand remove you hence;
> But rest for ever here: let *Egypt* give
> His Death that Peace, which it deny'd his Life.

Cleopatra's next speech is equally indebted to Daniel. Cleopatra is addressing the asp—

> Me thinkes I see, in now beholding thee.
> Better than Death, Deaths office thou dischargest,
> That with one gentle touch canst free our breath:
> And in a pleasing sleepe our soule inlargest,
> Making our selues not priuy to our death.
> O welcome now, of wonders wonder chiefe,
> That open canst with such an easie key
> The doore of life; come gentle cunning thiefe
> That from our selues so steal'st our selues away.

Dryden alters the order of the sentences and omits the rhymes, but he follows his original with extraordinary fidelity—

> Welcom, thou kind Deceiver!
> Thou best of Thieves; who, with an easie key,
> Do'st open Life, and unperceiv'd by us,
> Ev'n steal us from our selves: discharging so
> Death's dreadful Office better than himself,
> Touching our Limbs so gently into slumber,
> That Death stands by, deceiv'd by his own Image . . .

In the same speech in Daniel's play, Cleopatra continues—

> What now false flesh; what? and wilt thou conspire
> With *Cæsar* too, as thou wert none of ours . . .

and in Dryden's play, Cleopatra's next speech contains the lines—

> Coward Flesh—
> Would'st thou conspire with *Cæsar* to betray me,
> As thou wert none of mine? I'll force thee to 't,
> And not be sent by him,
> But bring my Self, my Soul to *Antony.*

Even the last lines of this passage contain echoes from *Cleopatra.*
Earlier in the play the heroine says—

> I must my selfe force open wide a dore
> To let out life, and so vnhouse my spirit . . .
> Ile bring my soule my selfe, and that with speede,
> My selfe will bring my soule to *Antony.*
>
> (IV.1160-85)

The next speech of Cleopatra in the fifth act contains the lines—

> Well, now this worke of mine is done, here ends
> This act of Life, that part the Fates assign'd; . . .
> Witnesse my soule parts free to *Antony,*
> And now prowde tyrant *Cæsar* doe thy worst.

The following is the corresponding passage in *All for Love*—

> Take hence; the work is done . . .
> *Cæsar,* thy worst;
> Now part us, if thou canst.

The question "Is this well done?" with Charmion's reply appears in
Plutarch as well as in the three dramatists. The last parallel occurs in
the last speech of *All for Love,* which echoes Charmion's words—

> And in this cheere th'impression of a smile,
> Did seeme to shew she skorns both death and *Cæsar* . . .

Dryden's Serapion says—

> Th'impression of a Smile left in her Face,
> Shows she dy'd pleas'd with him for whom she liv'd,
> And went to Charm him in another World.

The death-scene of Cleopatra is much more dramatic in *All for Love*
than in Daniel's play. Although Dryden borrows a great deal, he

achieves a greater power by compression and omission; but it cannot be said that line for line his echoes are superior to the Daniel originals. Daniel is led into occasional awkwardnesses by the difficulty of rhyme, but his language is purer than Dryden's, in whose play there are disturbing traces of the heroic style.

On the surface it appears that *All for Love* has greater unity than *Antony and Cleopatra;* but a study of the style, and particularly of the imagery of the two plays serves to show that Shakespeare's unity is deeper and more real than Dryden's, for it is a unity based on the poetic conception and expressed in a style, which, because it regards nothing as common or unclean is never led into bathos or bombast. Dryden's style is sometimes sublime, but it is more frequently rhetorical, sometimes bombastic, and occasionally flat. His imagery is at times commonplace and at times elaborate; it is frequently derived from Daniel and Shakespeare; and it is sometimes false. His images do not spring naturally from his theme, as the leaves from a tree; they are improvised; and though they may illuminate separate ideas, feelings, and even characters and scenes, they serve to destroy rather than to create the unity of the whole. *All for Love* is a fine tragedy decorated with poetry. It is not a poetic tragedy in the truest meaning of the term.

All for Love

by David Nichol Smith

We sometimes hear *All for Love* spoken of as if it were an attempt
to improve on Shakespeare. It was not that. It was an attempt to tell a
part of the story of *Antony and Cleopatra* in a different manner. 'I
have written against the Three Unities, I know that they are not necessary to a just drama, I know that they are not in the English tradition, but let me see what I can make of them': something like that
Dryden said to himself. The story had been dramatized in English
by others than Shakespeare—by Samuel Daniel, and Thomas May, and
Sir Charles Sedley (the Lisideius of the Essay *Of Dramatick Poesy*),
and their example, as Dryden tells us, gave him confidence 'to try
myself in the bow of Ulysses amongst the crowd of suitors'; but he was
urged on to telling it in a new manner by his reading of Racine's
latest play, *Phèdre,* for which apparently he did not greatly care. He
preferred Corneille to Racine. Familiar as he was with the French
drama, he did not like its drawing of character. He thought that Racine
had transformed the Hippolytus of Euripides into Monsieur Hippolyte.
Still *Phèdre* showed how the three Unities could be used, and, as all
the learned critics were saying, they had their warrant in the drama
of Greece and Rome. 'Mr. Rymer,' he remarks, 'has judiciously observed'—he did not always think him judicious—'that the Ancients are
and ought to be our masters.' Good and well! Now for an experiment!
And when *All for Love* is finished he says that 'the Unities of Time,
Place, and Action [are] more exactly observed than perhaps the English theatre requires.'

It is the observance of the Unity of Time that controls the differences from Shakespeare's play in subject, and characterization, and
pace, and color. If the action is to be confined to one day, and if the
play is to be a tragedy, the hero and heroine must be seen only in the
last day of their lives. French critics debated the length of the day.
One of them argued that as a play takes about three hours to perform,
the action of an ideal play would not extend beyond three hours, as

All for Love. *From part of the chapter "Plays" in* John Dryden *(Cambridge:
Cambridge University Press, 1950) by David Nichol Smith, pp. 140-43. Copyright ©
1950 by Cambridge University Press. Reprinted by permission of the publisher.*

if a representation of life should proceed at the same pace as real life. This was thought to be too exacting and twelve hours was proposed as a reasonable limit, but the general conclusion was that the time ought to be twenty-four hours with the option on rare occasions of thirty. It all seems rather absurd when put down in figures, but what is not absurd is the rule that the action ought to begin as near the catastrophe as the dramatist can contrive. The Unity of Time compelled Dryden to take only the concluding matter of Shakespeare's play—roughly what is found in the last two acts—and to expand that into a play of five acts. As a consequence there was a great reduction in the number of scenes and speaking parts—and, inevitably, a new Antony. Shakespeare's Antony must be a nobler character because we see him at the height of his power while Fortune was sometimes kind. His power is steadily sapped, yet we understand the devotion of his soldiers and the anxiety of his friends. He is ruined, and the magnificence of the ruin is impressed on us. But, because the action has to begin as near the catastrophe as is possible, we are never given the chance to admire Dryden's Antony. We see, and can see only, the Antony of the last phase, when he is the flickering ember of his glowing manhood. There was not the same reason for the inferiority of Dryden's Cleopatra. Shakespeare's is as great in death as in life, but age has begun to wither Dryden's. Passion has worn her. She has Antony in her toils, but she is in toils also, and when the end comes we are not moved as Shakespeare moves us. But Dryden's Cleopatra is well drawn, and is more within the range of ordinary experience.

All for Love is a sombre play in comparison with Shakespeare's, which is suffused with the splendor of the Mediterranean sun. Of all Shakespeare's dramas none has so bright a coloring as *Antony and Cleopatra*. I would not suggest that Dryden could have given us the same sense of light and warmth, but he had to adopt a different color scheme—from the very beginning he had to tone his color to the impending catastrophe because he was to tell us what happened on one tragic day, because he was conforming to the Unity of Time.

It is Dryden's best play. He knew that, with the aid of Shakespeare, he had risen above his normal level in the drama. 'I hope I may affirm, and without vanity, that by imitating him, I have excelled myself throughout the play.' He says 'imitating him,' but he means following him and thinking of his example. In passages he did definitely imitate; he worked on many of Shakespeare's ideas and descriptions. But the play is not an imitation. It is a transmutation by a gifted artist who knew his powers and their limits. To call it a triumph of craftsmanship, which it certainly is, may be to suggest only a triumph in the rehandling of substance that is available in methods that are known. But Dryden used a tool of his own devising—his own blank

verse. That is the great innovation in *All for Love*. Again he gives
Shakespeare the credit. 'In my style I have professed to imitate the
divine Shakespeare; which that I might perform more freely, I have
disencumbered myself from rhyme.' But his blank verse is not Shakespeare's. He cites the passage which he liked best, and a portion of it
I must quote. Ventidius has come to urge Antony to action, and
Antony replies—

> I know thy meaning.
> But I have lost my Reason, have disgrac'd
> The name of Soldier, with inglorious ease;
> In the full Vintage of my flowing honors,
> Sat still, and saw it prest by other hands.
> Fortune came smiling to my youth, and woo'd it,
> And purple greatness met my ripen'd years.
> When first I came to Empire, I was born
> On Tides of People, crouding to my Triumphs;
> The wish of Nations; and the willing World
> Receiv'd me as its pledge of future peace;
> I was so great, so happy, so belov'd,
> Fate could not ruine me; till I took pains
> And work'd against my Fortune, chid her from me,
> And turn'd her loose; yet still she came again.
> My careless dayes, and my luxurious nights,
> At length have weary'd her, and now she's gone,
> Gone, gone, divorc'd for ever. Help me, Soldier,
> To curse this Mad-man, this industrious Fool,
> Who labour'd to be wretched: pr'ythee curse me.

I quote this passage the more readily as so far I have quoted only
rhymed verse. Let us ask ourselves this question—Who since Dryden
has written better blank verse in the drama?

Dryden in Egypt: Reflections on *All for Love*

by Norman Suckling

The question has been asked many times why, when England produced a comedy of manners comparable, though not parallel, to that of Molière, we can point to no such achievement in the realm of tragedy; why the English heroic tragedy of the Restoration period cannot well be named in the same breath as the French theatre rendered illustrious by Corneille and Racine. The widely differing tone set by the two countries' respective courts will not explain the whole matter, nor even the break in tradition caused by the closing of the theatres under the Commonwealth. The new dramatic form known as opera was received with sufficient readiness in Restoration England for a similar welcome to have been possible for that *spoken opera* which is classical tragedy; but for all that, this latter took little hold. One play however there is which, though doubtless not as great as the masterpieces of Corneille and Racine, is at least worthy to stand in their company: Dryden's *All for Love,* that remarkable work variously acclaimed as a homage to Shakespeare and decried as a proof of its author's inferior measure, but better understood as a triumphant essay in a *genre* quite different from that consecrated by the older dramatist —whose reputation in Dryden's time was high without being obsessive, and whose example might be quoted to support a new writer but hardly to crush him. I wish in these few pages to suggest that the quality of *All for Love,* as representing a different but equally interesting dramatic *genre* from that of *Antony and Cleopatra,* is of greater importance than the fact that it was written by a lesser poet.

A spoken opera, I have said; and it is true that classical tragedy is distinguished by a kind of lyrical declamation so carefully ordered that the whole is (as Paul Valéry put it with regard to opera itself) "homogène, ou également distant de la vie en tous ses moyens de production." [1] One result of this principle of equidistance is, of course,

---

"Dryden in Egypt: Reflections on All for Love*" by Norman Suckling. From the* Durham University Journal, *XLV, No. 1 (December, 1952), 2-7. Copyright © by the* Durham University Journal. *Reprinted by permission of the University of Durham. Slightly abridged for this edition.*

[1] *Histoire d' Amphion,* in *Variété, III,* p. 88.

that classical tragedy abandons everything in the way of "comic" or "low" relief, because to introduce it would disturb the perspective in which life is regarded by this kind of tragedy. And I am not at all sure that anything of value is lost by the sacrifice. I should prefer *Antony and Cleopatra* without the interlude of the Clown who brings the basket of fruit containing the asps. I could never see that such fooling on an altogether different poetic level contributed anything to the tragic effect of the scenes flanking it; it profits us not at all to be so violently shifted from one to another focus on reality. And I find it quite impossible to share Saintsbury's preference for "the greater freedom of the chronicle-play" over "the artificial tragedy of situation." From the aspect under which the success of a work of art is due to factors other than the individual genius of its author, the best examples of the chronicle-play seem to me to succeed in spite of their *genre*, the tragedy of situation because of it; the freedom of the chronicle-play is for the most part the freedom of aimlessness, the freedom of a chemical substance wandering in a void.

Shakespeare's excellences above Dryden are those of a greater individual genius, not of a superior dramatic kind; when indeed they are not a matter of Shakespeare's power over a kind of poetry peculiar, almost, to him. He will exercise his unique gift of combining the tragic with the pathetic—where most other writers would become either maudlin or stilted—in such supreme moments of lyrical declamation as

> Unarm, Eros, the long day's task is done

or will point such moments by a particularly glowing piece of imagery:

> Downy windows, close,
> And golden Phoebus never be beheld
> Of eyes again so royal! Your crown's awry;
> I'll mend it, and then play.

This is not the poetry of which Dryden was capable; but it was not the kind of tragedy in which he worked that prevented him from scaling heights of an equal poetic elevation, though of a different poetic principle. His verse is not so much *lacking* in "high lights" as constructed on a principle which does not call for them; nevertheless within the framework of his chosen kind he could produce, not the Shakespearean imagery (which is not what he was trying after), but a line which, like the key-lines of Corneille or Racine, has so finally summed up a situation, or an aspect of one, and penetrated so unerringly to its barest essentials, as to express it in words which are to the last degree *justes* without being *rares*. Under the influence of Shakespeare, the Romantics and the Hebrew Prophets, said Lytton Strachey, we have come to be-

lieve that poetry apart from *le mot rare* is an impossibility; and he
pointed to Racine as evidence to the contrary:

> Tais-toi, perfide,
> Et n'impute qu'à toi ton lâche parricide . . .
> Mais parlez. De son sort qui t'a rendu l'arbitre?
> Pourquoi l'assassiner? Qu'a-t-il fait? A quel titre?
> *Qui te l'a dit?*

But in this one play of Dryden's also, at least, there are passages which
illustrate the same possibility of poetry with an uncolored vocabulary:

> My lord looks down concerned, and fears my stay,
> Lest I should be surprised.
> Keep him not waiting for his love too long.

Uncolored also are the externals of Dryden's setting; the pageantry of
the Egyptian palace may have afforded his scenic assistants an oppor-
tunity for a ballet-interlude in the coronation of Antony, but he deliberately avoids the verbal splendors whereby the Elizabethan dramatist would compensate for the physical absence of such things. We have
no sumptuous account of Cleopatra's barge, "like a burnished throne,"
nor of feasting in Egypt; or at any rate, we have it only in restricted
terms, subordinate always to its function in dramatic development.
Dryden's description of Cleopatra in her state is pale by the side of
Shakespeare's, but it is more closely tied to its purpose—that of re-
awakening in Dolabella, all unintentionally on Antony's part, a dormant passion for her:

> To soft flutes
> The silver oars kept time; and while they played,
> The hearing gave new pleasure to the sight,
> And both to thought. 'Twas heaven, or somewhat more; . . .
> Then, Dolabella, where was then thy soul?
> Was not thy fury quite disarmed with wonder?

Neither is there in Dryden the profusion of personages whereby *Antony
and Cleopatra* manifests a point in common with the tradition set by
Marlowe with his stage-full of kings. The cast of *All for Love* is as small
as that of any Cornelian tragedy, and the parallel extends even to the
fact that one or two of the characters assume functions similar to those
of the classical confidant. Not indeed to the extent of being mere
mirrors as the French confidants sometimes are; but it is instructive
in this respect to examine Dryden's Alexas, who combines in his own
person the two Shakespearean figures of Alexas and Mardian and is,
if anything, more essential to the action than either of these two in

Shakespeare. In particular he fulfills a function not always noticed in confidants and not, of course, necessary for all of them: that of absorbing some of the odium which might otherwise attach to certain actions of a personage for whom it is important to preserve sympathy. We find this in Aufidius' advice to Perpenna in Corneille's *Sertorius,* and in the relation obtaining between Maxime and his freedman Euphorbe in *Cinna,* to which an extra point is given by the description of Euphorbe as an *affranchi* and not simply a *confident*—the reputation of freedmen being what it was. And there are still more illustrious examples: Racine's Phèdre is similarly able to shift some of the blame for her perfidy upon "la détestable Œnone," and it is noteworthy that Euripides provided her with an ancient precedent for so doing by his presentation of the Nurse in *Hippolytus.* Dryden's Alexas is a character of this kind, and he absorbs much more odium than anyone can do for Shakespeare's Cleopatra, who is not—and this is a central matter—intended to be taken as the type of a *lover,* proper, at all.

It is remarkable how small a place love occupies in the tragic consciousness of Shakespeare; apart from the brilliant exception of *Romeo and Juliet* it hardly enters into his great tragedies. *Othello* is concerned not with love but with jealousy—a very different thing—and *Antony and Cleopatra* is not a tragedy of love at all, but of infatuation and coquetry, *until* the last act. For, even if Antony may properly be said to love Cleopatra, he does not thereby make her a worthy object of affection; in spite of Fr. D'Arcy,[2] love—even the purest—cannot create value in its object. The existence of love in any sense that can justify (as certainly neither infatuation nor jealousy can do) the aura of nobility attaching to the word, depends on conditions offered by the object as well as the subject. The devotion wasted on an unresponsive object is hardly to be called love; certainly not if the word is to refer in the first and most central place to the love of those who realize themselves by the discovery of essential and distinctive humanity in each other. If the passion which manifests itself as jealousy, as possessiveness or as abject surrender is to be called love, then another name must be found for the love of friends, of beauty or of God—and, for that matter, for the spiritual (as distinct from the "passionate" or "transported") love of man and woman: with which the "dark passion," noted and keenly analyzed in our day by Mr. C. S. Lewis, Fr. D'Arcy and M. Denis de Rougemont, has nothing in common except its being rooted in sexual desire, a mould from which many roots of varying natures may draw their sustenance. I am not decrying the devotion of a self-sacrificing mother or of a soldier who dies for his Emperor, but only pointing out that even this is not the

<hr>

[2] *The Mind and Heart of Love,* p. 70.

same with the realization, at once mutual and of self, apparent to lovers proper, whose existence is so fully explainable in terms of each other that the question of sacrifice is not pertinent, because the correspondence between the feeling of each and the reality of the other is so complete.

The amorous code of the Précieuses has earned a place of ridicule in literary history, but it is sometimes forgotten that the familiar modern conception of passion for its own sake (sometimes amounting to no more than sensibility for its own sake) is radically the same thing; and that neither it nor the "dark passion," the ineluctable possession of Racinian tragedy ("Vénus toute entière à sa proie attachée") is truly to be called love in the sense I have indicated. This love which fulfils itself in complete understanding is, to begin with, more within the scope and the capacity of those for whom love begins with sensuality than of those for whom it is either Quinaultian highfalutin or Racinian "possession." It is indeed almost inconceivable without an externalization in physical communion, and at the same time is none the less spiritual for that. ("Then is love lust?" asked Héloise of Gilles de Vannes; and Gilles replied:

> Its root is lust . . . But the rose is lovelier than its root, Héloise. And by your leave, madam, a rose grows better in a dunghill than in a quarry of white Carrara marble. And dies . . . less soon.[3]

It is on this ground that Dryden's play is saved from being of no more relevance to reality than the *précieux* plays and romances of the *Astrée* succession, as it might otherwise have been; for, though in the respects detailed above, and others, it is the greatest—perhaps the only great—classical tragedy in English, yet its theme is neither Cornelian nor Racinian, but suggests rather the amorous tragedy of the kind that delighted the *ruelles*—a resemblance from which it is saved mainly by its avoidance of all false "spirituality." "The world well lost for love" is a sentiment typical of neither Corneille nor Racine; partly because both were concerned with something more akin to "dark passion" than to a love for which the world *would* be well lost. Corneille always sets over against love something to be regarded as preferable—usually one form or another of honor; Racine presents it simply as a worker of havoc. But Dryden, if he does not draw on the same sources of tragedy as the two great French dramatists, nevertheless escapes the unreality of the *pre*-classical writers of tragedy and tragi-comedy by giving us a Cleopatra for whom one would indeed be ready to lose the world—a treatment of his heroine for which he had few precedents in previous drama, certainly not in Shakespeare.

3 Helen Waddell, *Peter Abelard*, pp. 25-6.

For Shakespeare's Cleopatra does not love Antony at all, until the last act. A real love could be attributed to her only by those who are so unaware of the truth of the matter as to suppose that love is compatible with coquetry. Shakespeare's Cleopatra is a coquette—Professor Bonamy Dobrée has called her "a flashy vulgarian." She is more concerned with her power over Antony than with his happiness or his honor; always until the last act, when a realization of the irrevocable end rouses her to unsurpassed lyric heights and to a genuine love too late, as it comes to so many of us. I should not like to state categorically that this is the more frequent type of woman, but it is the type that attracted more of Shakespeare's attention, to the extent of encouraging in some of his critics the suggestion that in his portrayal of this type he was drawing on his own experience. That was the point of Miss Clemence Dane's play of *Will Shakespeare*—to present the poet in the toils of a woman who was capable of love only on exceptional occasions, and to show him as so affected by this experience that it colored most of the feminine portraits he drew. But Dryden's Cleopatra is a very different character, and may be said genuinely to love Antony, not merely to exploit him. She had deserted at Actium, but there is no reason to doubt her own statement that her flight was due to simple fear. She has genuinely refused Octavius' offer, where the Cleopatra of Shakespeare would have used it as a stake in her game (and in fact begins to do something of the kind in her scene with Octavius' messenger Thidias). We need not, doubtless, take at its face value her statement that

> Nature meant me
> A wife, a silly, harmless, household dove,
> But Fortune, that has made a mistress of me,
> Has thrust me out to the wide world, unfurnished
> Of falsehood to be happy

and if there were no other option than to explain her in terms of the two types noted by Valéry, the *matrone essentielle* and the *danseuse-née*—with regard to whom it is important not to fall into the error of trying to seduce the former or marrying the latter [4]—one would hesitate to qualify her exclusively as the *matrone!* But neither is she at all recognizably the *danseuse;* certainly she is not compounded all of feminine wile and power-hunger like her Shakespearean counterpart. The only time she stoops to the coquette's trick of arousing jealousy it is by Alexas' suggestion, and what is more she does not do it at all cleverly. The scene is vitiated a little by Dryden's making her accept the sentimental convention that "jealousy's a proof of love"—whereas in reality

[4] *Autres Rhumbs* in *Tel Quel II,* p. 182.

they exclude each other—but it is clear that in embarking on this line
of policy she is acting against her own nature. Shakespeare's Cleopatra
on the other hand would have found no difficulty in it, and would not
moreover have needed the promptings of her counselor to suggest it—
those promptings whereby, as I have indicated, Alexas in Dryden absorbs the odium of the action. Later in the play it is again Alexas who
(to save his own "bacon" as much as Cleopatra's) feigns her death,
unknown to her; but in Shakespeare the same development is presented as of Cleopatra's own invention—or, at any rate, with no more
than a word from Charmian—and it is she who deliberately instructs
Mardian to "word it piteously."

Dryden's Cleopatra has in fact shed most of the features of her
traditional "serpentine" character and acquired many of those of the
lover who is a fulfilment rather than a fatality to him whom she loves;
without, one must admit, being in any way quotable as a partner in
Christian marriage. There is indeed a certain ambiguity evident
throughout Dryden's play in his simultaneous exploitation of "official"
sympathy for Octavia as a lawful wife and of Cleopatra's scorn for
"that thing, that dull insipid lump." The one can clearly count on as
ready a predisposition in the audience as the other, and can do so in
our own day as well as in Dryden's own. We should in fact find it
difficult nowadays to attach even as much weight as Dryden did to
the fact that the love of Antony and Cleopatra was "illicit"—which
may point, according to one's predilections, to the triumph in modern
times of M. de Rougemont's "myth" of love outside morality, or to a
recognition of the nature of genuine love as unrelated (like all other
ultimately precious states of mind) to any finalities of social ethics or
survival-values. But at least Dryden has pointed the way to a consciousness of the love which, working outside the framework of social
morality and therefore as likely to be manifested in the absence as
under the sanction of the marriage-bond, offers those who are capable
of it the prospect of recognizing and realizing their highest nature—
as against the obscure satisfaction of uneasy stirrings for their own sake
which, as M. de Rougemont noted, the devotees of "dark passion"
wilfully stimulate to their own undoing.

For Dryden's lovers give more than one indication, in the course of
his play, of having approached well within sight of the love which is
evinced by understanding rather than conflict, by *l'agrément et l'accord*
rather than by "constantly overcoming or surrendering to each other,"
by serenity rather than anxiety,—the love which does not touch Shakespeare's Cleopatra until the logic of events has brought her to the
beginnings of what might have been love too late. Admittedly the
serenity is not evident in the *péripéties* of Dryden's play; but even the
Dolabella episode shows on Cleopatra's part a genuine desire to *keep*

Antony, not to put him on the rack of uncertainty as to whether she
is wholly his or no. And the elegiac tone of Antony's final retrospect
on their history is far removed from the frustration of passion:

> Think we have had a clear and glorious day,
> And Heaven did kindly to delay the storm
> Just till our close of evening.

Such, he says, has been their love until his "last disastrous times" that
they do not need to regret a moment of their ten years together. For
this love the world is well lost indeed, which it would not be, had their
relation been what it is for the tormented figures of Racine and what
we have every reason to suppose it was before, as well as during the
play, for the Antony and Cleopatra of Shakespeare, with whom a period of agreement could hardly at any time have been more than an
uneasy truce. The question at issue in Shakespeare is, will Antony lose
the world for one who (until it is too late) is not worth his losing it?
the question in Dryden, will Antony, for the sake of another duty
(whether to Rome or to Octavia) abandon a genuine love? And it is
here, I suggest, that we may find the greatness of *All for Love*. The
play is not properly to be described as a variation on Shakespeare at
all, but rather as an employment of Shakespearean prosody to a very
different purpose. Those features of the plot which correspond with
Shakespeare are explainable mostly as borrowings from a common
historical original; and I am willing to maintain that in the one
place where Dryden has transferred some of Shakespeare's language—
in Charmion's valediction:

> Yes, 'tis well done, and like a queen, the last
> Of her great race

he has improved on it by avoiding the tautology of "royal kings." His
own acknowledgements to Shakespeare in his preface are rather to a
master than a source, returning thanks rather for a model of blank
verse than for contributions to a dramatic ethic. It is in this latter
direction however that Dryden is significant. He presents a love which
is neither *précieux* nor possessive, and shows signs, however incom-
plete, of understanding that lovers are none the less lovers if their
profit in each other is such as to make them (for a time, and apart
from external obstacles) happy. Shakespeare gives us this nowhere
but in *Romeo and Juliet,* and for most of us the urgent spectacle of
corroding passion renders it a remote prospect indeed. But we may be
grateful to the dramatist in whose work it so much as begins to be
apparent that the road to glory is through suffering only by the per-
versity of our fate; that we are betrayed, especially in our relations
with those dearest to us, not only—as in the theory of Aristotle and the

practice of the French tragedians—"by what is false within," but by what operates from without against the best that is in us, often enough (witness Ventidius, Octavia and even Dolabella) by identifying itself with what is best in others; that the anxious tension characterizing so many of our personal relations has nothing to recommend it in itself; and that only the love which is *not* a disrupting passion has any title to be regarded as so noble a thing that for it the world would be well lost.

Intention and Achievement in *All for Love*

by *Everett H. Emerson, Harold E. Davis,*
and Ira Johnson

All for Love "has one fault equal to many . . . that, by admitting the romantic omnipotence of love," Dryden "has recommended, as laudable and worthy of imitation that conduct, which, through all ages, the good have censured as vicious, and the bad despised as foolish." This criticism of Dryden's masterpiece by Dr. Johnson (*Lives,* ed. Hill, 1905, I, 361) has received less attention than it deserves, for it points out an important confusion between Dryden's intention and his achievement, and it leads to a re-evaluation which demonstrates other basic discrepancies.

Dryden declared in his preface to the tragedy that he was attracted to the subject by the "excellency of the moral"; that the "chief persons represented were famous patterns of unlawful love; and their end accordingly was unfortunate." For Dryden the love affair of Antony and Cleopatra contained good potentials for tragedy because it exemplified punishment for a love "founded upon vice"; it made virtue attractive and vice repellent, and therefore met the requirement for poetic justice. But Dryden was aware of some of the weaknesses in this ready-made moral exemplum: he believed that the lovers do not demand full tragic pity because "the crimes of love, which they both committed, were not occasioned by any necessity, or fatal ignorance, but were wholly voluntary; since our passions are, or ought to be, within our power" (*Essays*, ed. Ker, 1900 I, 191-192). The inevitability of tragedy is lacking, according to Dryden, since the lovers are not forced into their actions. But if we look closely at the play, we find that it does not present a picture of "the crimes of love" and of unlawful lovers being punished for their voluntary transgressions. Instead, it gives us almost the opposite: a love that is inevitable, an uncontrollable force; and the lovers vindicated because of their passion. Our sym-

"*Intention and Achievement in* All for Love" *by Everett H. Emerson, Harold E. Davis, and Ira Johnson. From* College English, *XVII (1955), 84-7. Copyright © 1955 by the National Council of Teachers of English. Reprinted with the permission of the National Council of Teachers of English and Everett H. Emerson, Harold E. Davis, and Ira Johnson.*

pathies are drawn to the lovers and held there because their passions are not within their power. At least from this point of view Dryden builded better than he knew.

The theme of *All for Love* is the conflict of reason and honor with passion in the form of illicit love. From the preface it seems that Dryden wished to show how Antony, torn between these two, chooses unreasonable, passionate love and is consequently punished for his denial of reason. Let us see how Dryden presented this conflict in the play itself.

At the beginning of Act I, the struggle is evident. Antony, "Unbent, unsinew'd, made a Womans Toy / Shrunk from the vast extent of all his honours," hopes to "cure his mind of Love." Ventidius, the "old true-stampt Roman," sides with the world of reason, of "plainness, fierceness, rugged virtue," by cursing the joy and revelry of the Egyptians, and by deriding Alexas, the eunuch (the "unmanned") as "Antony's other fate" (*Works*, ed. Summers, 1932, IV, 192, 194-196). Aware of his degradation, Antony admits the truth of Ventidius's charges:

> . . . I have lost my reason, have disgrac'd
> The name of Soldier, with inglorious ease.
> In the full Vintage of my flowing honors,
> Sate still, and saw it prest by other hands. (p. 199)

When Antony resolves to kill himself because the world is not worth keeping, Ventidius offers to die with him. Thus, early in the play some of the contradictions are evident. Although Ventidius argues for reason, he wants to do an unreasonable thing because of his deep love for Antony. In terms of the morality of Dryden's preface, Ventidius' idea is wrong; in the context of the play itself, it seems admirable. We thus have between intention and achievement a split, which, though minor, presages more serious difficulties.

At the close of Act I, Ventidius' persuasion is temporarily victorious, and Antony returns to reason and honor: he declares to Ventidius: "Our hearts and armes are still the same" (p. 203).

In Act II appears Cleopatra, Antony's love and his ruin, who attempts to bring Antony back into her world. The opening and closing lines of the act indicate the progress of the action and her success:

> *Cleopatra.* What shall I do, or whither shall I turn?
> Ventidius has o'rcome, and he will go.
> . . . (p. 204)
> *Antony.* How I long for night!
> That both the sweets of mutual love may try. (p. 216)

But Cleopatra is far more than the evil temptress, offering ruin, that Dryden seems to indicate in his preface: instead, she illustrates a moral complexity which reason cannot solve.

> *Iras.* Call reason to assist you.
> *Cleopatra.*   I have none.
> And none would have: my Love's a noble madness,
> Which shows the cause deserv'd it. Moderate sorrow
> Fits vulgar Love, and for a vulgar Man:
> But I have lov'd with such transcendent passion,
> I soar'd, at first quite out of Reasons view,
> And now am lost above it. (p. 204)

Her transcendent love—comparable to Ventidius' love for Antony—is not the negation of reason, but an emotion which rises *above* it.

In Act II Alexas speaks as the man of unimpassioned reason:

> You [Cleopatra] misjudge;
> You see through Love, and that deludes your sight:
> As what is strait, seems crooked through the Water;
> But I, who bear my reason undisturb'd
> Can see this Antony . . . (p. 206)

Our undisturbed man of reason, is ironically, "unmanned," a eunuch; and if this speech is designed to identify him with reason, then his later failures—his counsels to Cleopatra in Act V to negotiate with Caesar, his lie to Antony, his scheme to make Antony jealous—have the effect of discrediting reason. He "sees through reason" and *his* sight is deluded.

With the introduction of Octavia in Act III Dryden feared that "the compassion she moved to herself and children was destructive to that which I reserved for Antony and Cleopatra" (*Essays*, I, 192). The passage indicates that Dryden regarded Octavia as a sympathetic character who would arouse compassion. But it hardly seems an accident that Octavia, the incarnation of honor, is so well drawn as a "respectable" woman, because it is her pride, her regard for honor in the form of her reputation, which qualifies her "love" as something far more of a vice than the love of Antony and Cleopatra. Octavia is so undeniably self-righteous—and it is difficult to believe that she would not have seemed so to a Restoration audience—that Antony does what any man would do when he returns to Cleopatra in Act V. A good illustration of Octavia's morality is her plea:

> Go to him. Children, go;
> Kneel to him, take him by the hand, speak to him:
> For you may speak, and he may own you too,

> Without a blush; and so he cannot all
> His Children: go, I say, and pull him to me,
> And pull him to your selves, from that bad Woman.
> You, Agrippina, hang upon his arms;
> And you, Antonia, clasp about his waist:
> If he will shake you off, if he will dash you
> Against the Pavement, you must bear it, Children;
> For you are mine, and I was born to suffer. (p. 226)

Here, Antony, the Roman conqueror of worlds, and passionate, mature lover, is being chided by a virtuous wife (who, to Shakespeare, was a "statue rather than a breather"), and being checked in such a way that he loses not only his dignity but also his masculine honor. This sudden intrusion of "virtue" into the scene may be morally necessary, but Dryden makes it so much less attractive than the compelling physical love affair that he is obviously aligning himself with passion and against the reason and virtue he urges in his preface.

Even the sophisticated "serpent of the Nile" is dampened by this overbearing virtue and becomes a pale shadow of Octavia:

> *Cleopatra.*   I have suffer'd more.
> You bear the specious Title of a Wife,
> To guild your Cause, and draw the pitying World
> To favour it: the World condemns poor me;
> For I have lost my Honour, lost my Fame,
> And stain'd the glory of my Royal House,
> And all to bear the branded Name of Mistress,
> There wants but life, and that too I would lose
> For him I love. (p. 229)

She feels wronged and pities herself. Dryden seems to have struggled to give Cleopatra some of the "nobility" of the wronged Octavia. But the effort was unsuccessful; Cleopatra's false cloak of virtue does not enrich her personality but detracts from her essential character of mature sophistication: she is hardly a woman who would mourn the loss of honor through love. She loves, we remember, with a "transcendent passion." This desperate, illicit love of Antony, a world-weary Roman, and the beautiful, sensual, and cunning Cleopatra has so enmeshed them that they are unable to control themselves, although both are well aware of what they are doing. So wholly outside this passion are Octavia's middle-class morality and Cleopatra's attempt to echo it that their behaviour is not tragic but maudlin.

In Act V Dryden seems to have been faced once and for all with the choice of punishing his lovers and proving the "excellency of the moral" or closing the play with the victory over reason and honor which has been inevitable since the first act. Antony's closing lines indicate that Dryden abandoned altogether his ideal of poetic justice:

> Ten years love,
> And not a moment lost, but all improv'd
> To th' utmost joys: What Ages have we liv'd?
> And now to die each others; and, so dying,
> While hand in hand we walk in Groves below,
> Whole Troops of Lovers Ghosts shall flock about us,
> And all the Train be ours. (p. 258)

No speech after this suggests a moral condemnation of the lovers. Rather the play ends on quite another note:

> And Fame, to late Posterity, shall tell,
> No lovers liv'd so great, or dy'd so well. (p. 261)

Faced with the opposing viewpoints of Dryden's preface on the one hand and the play itself with its sub-title on the other, we had best take *The World Well Lost* as the more accurate statement of Dryden's intention.

In his preface Dryden informed his readers that his intention was to "follow the practice of the ancients" (*Essays*, I, 200), to adhere to neoclassical concepts of tragedy. But once again Dryden was at odds with his intention; although *All for Love* is certainly correct in terms of the physical properties of classical tragedy (or at least Dryden's understanding of them), the play does not provide a true tragic catharsis. Although it would be an error to rely too completely upon a comparison, an examination of the immediate cause of the tragedy as compared with that in Shakespeare's *Antony and Cleopatra* can be useful in illustrating this weakness of *All for Love*. We should not judge Dryden's play a failure because it does not do things that Shakespeare's does; it is a different play, conceived with considerable different dramatic intentions. But in both plays the lovers die, and die within the dramatic framework of the tragedy.

In Shakespeare's play the tragedy of Antony and Cleopatra is brought about almost wholly by the love affair; all through the play we feel the awful compulsion of this love forcing them to their inevitable end. Dryden gave to the early part of his play the same impression of inexorability (even though he failed to recognize it, if we can believe his preface). But the destruction later of Antony and Cleopatra is not occasioned by their love alone. Instead, the motivation for their deaths, the quarrel which leads to the suicide of Antony, is the result of the blundering lies and machinations of the well-meaning Alexas, who is not directly involved in the love affair. Specifically, it is his lie to Antony about Cleopatra's death which causes Antony to kill himself and later Cleopatra to do the same. Although there is a similar chain of events in Shakespeare's play, there Cleopatra agrees to Charmian's subterfuge (hiding in the monument, the false suicide); whereas in *All for Love* Alexas on his own initiative tells the lie which sets off the chain of forces. Thus he assumes the immediate responsibility for the deaths, which are not the inevitable result of the love affair but the result of a casual mischance (the mistake due, ironically, to Alexas' faith in reason). The action moves from the lovers' entangling themselves in inexorable fate to a simple accident, not caused by the lovers themselves.

We might stretch our credulity considerably and try to see Alexas as the perpetrator of poetic justice, the "punishment" inflicted upon the lovers. But then the whole problem of sympathies and motivations in the play becomes confused because Alexas is the least sympathetic character in the play and is, as such, a poor instrument of justice. Further, as we have seen, the lovers are hardly punished: "No lovers liv'd so great, or dy'd so well." The only clear assumption we can be left with is that Alexas' lies are a dramatic weakness.

The question of where Dryden's sympathies were in the one work which he wrote for his own satisfaction may be a key to the split which we have observed between Dryden's intentions and his achievements. Dryden believed that Antony and Cleopatra should be punished since they violated one of the basic strictures of his age, but yet, as we have seen, he could not regard his tragic hero and heroine as illustrations of a neo-classical moral maxim—for *his* lovers, the world was "well lost." The result was a conflict, to which the central weaknesses in *All for Love* may be attributed.

Yet the play is not altogether unsuccessful: it has moments of grandeur and some of Dryden's most intense poetry; some have even believed that if Shakespeare had never written, it would be one of the most impressive monuments of English drama. Perhaps so. But this study suggests that the play is full of confusions: the conclusion of the play endorses passionate love, though earlier in the play, and in the preface, passionate love is condemned as unreasonable and therefore immoral; the inevitability of the action is marred because the catastrophe is brought about by an accident; the role of reason in the play is ambiguous. Clearly the play is not what it has been called (by Dobrée, *Restoration Tragedy,* 1929, p. 90): a play which "has a coherence, a direction to one end, in a word, a unity."

Ideal Form in *All for Love*

by Jean H. Hagstrum

If we wish to examine Dryden's ideal general nature, we must, since he wrote no epic, turn to *All for Love,* the work that he said he wrote for himself alone. In a subtle passage in the "Parallel of Poetry and Painting" Dryden compares this play to the *Oedipus,* to which he contributed only two acts. In the *Oedipus* he had improved upon nature, following Sophocles in drawing men as they ought to be. But in *All for Love,* the idealization, though present, was less extreme; it had "nothing of outrageous panegyrick." The passions of the hero and heroine

> were their own, and such as were given them by history; only the deformities of them were cast into shadows, that they might be the objects of compassion: whereas if I had chosen a noon-day light for them, somewhat must have been discovered, which would rather have moved our hatred than our pity.

We are not now interested in the exact degree of idealization present in this play. We are interested in the analogy with painting, here only implied by the metaphor of light and shade but elsewhere obviously drawn and clearly applied to the art of tragedy.

In fact, of the many correspondences that exist between poetry and painting, none is closer, Dryden believed, than that between a tragedy and a historical painting. Both share the problem of ennobling the form without destroying the resemblance to history. And a disciplined tragedy like *All for Love,* which attempts to respect the three dramatic unities, strives to attain the simultaneousness and instantaneousness of painting. The author of a tragedy and the painter of a historical scene both face the difficult task of imposing severe formal economy upon grand and heroic action. The parallel with painting is valid, Dryden conceded, also for the epic, but it is "more complete to tragedy." This is because "Tragedy and Picture are more narrowly circumscrib'd by the mechanic rules of time and place, than the epic poem." So smitten was Dryden with the closeness of this parallel that he gave extreme statement to the pictorialist ideal. Since economy is an artistic desideratum, "I must give the advantage of painting, even above tragedy, that what this last represents in the space of so many hours, the former shews us in one moment." Of Poussin's "Institution of the Blessed Sacrament" he said:

> Here is one but indivisible point of time observed; but one action performed by so many persons in one room, and at the same table; yet the eye cannot comprehend at once the whole object, nor the mind follow it so fast; it is considered at leisure, and seen by intervals. Such are the subjects of noble pictures; and such are only to be undertaken by noble hands.

Dryden has in this passage clearly stated the ideal of the neoclassical picturesque. That ideal exalted the "single moment" of painting and invited literary art to strive to achieve it. This notion of the close parallel between the tragic drama and historical painting, between pictorial economy and the rules of drama, did not, of course, begin or end with Dryden.[1] But he seems to have been greatly attracted by the neoclassical picturesque,[2] a fact that alerts us to the striking pictorial quality of *All for Love,* which arises in part from a stricter adherence to the dramatic unities than, as Dryden said in the Preface, is required for the English stage. This quality appears not absolutely but relatively. One must consider what a play can be, what other plays on this very theme have been—restlessly varied by changing scenes, warring characters, melodramatic actions, and innumerable personages—to appreciate how pictorially static Dryden's play actually is. The characters tend to be fixed in poses. Antony turns to the right; he turns to the left; he turns finally to death and Cleopatra. The actions may be

---

[1] Testelin, Dufresnoy, Boileau, Coypel, Webb, Jouin, and Jonathan Richardson all stressed the especial closeness of tragedy and painting and the relation of the unities to painting [see *Laokoön: Lessing, Herder, Goethe,* ed. William Guild Howard (New York, 1910), pp. lx ff.].

[2] Dryden states it elsewhere, in "To Sir Godfrey Kneller," thus: If you were not occupied with portraits, we should

> ". . . see your noble pencil trace
> Our unities of action, time, and place;
> A whole compos'd of parts, and those the best,
> With ev'ry various character express'd;
> Heroes at large, and at a nearer view;
> Less, and at distance, an ignobler crew;
> While all the figures in one action join,
> As tending to complete the main design." (ll. 166-73).

significant, but they are extremely slight. The speeches of the characters resemble noble inscriptions or mottoes—an effect that Shakespeare achieves in his final death scene but that is present all through
Dryden's play. The speeches in *All for Love* are often iconic. One
character describes another as if he were a work of art and not a living
being. Ventidius says of—and to—Antony:

> But you, ere love misled your wandering eyes,
> Were sure the chief and best of human race,
> Framed in the very pride and boast of nature;
> So perfect, that the gods, who formed you, wondered
> At their own skill, and cried—A lucky hit
> Has mended our design. Their envy hindered,
> Else you had been immortal, and a pattern,
> When Heaven would work for ostentation's sake
> To copy out again (Act I, Sc. 1).

The words "framed," "perfect," "skill," "hit," "design," "pattern,"
and "copy" all are signs that a graphic metaphor is operative, that
Antony is being viewed as a work of ideal art. We attempted to demonstrate in our last chapter that the analogy with statuary was often
present when a neoclassical poet sought to idealize his forms. The
point is illustrated here.

It is so important in Dryden and in the neoclassical poetry that
followed him that it must be more fully developed. In the "Parallel"
Dryden sees a close correspondence between pictorial posture and epic
description: "The posture of a poetic figure is . . . the description
of [the] heroes in the performance of such or such an action . . ." To
illustrate this Dryden turns to Vergil, to the scene in the tenth book
of the *Aeneid* in which Aeneas slays Lausus, who is defending his
father, the Etruscan king Mezentius. Of this scene Dryden says:

> [Aeneas] considers Lausus rescuing his father at the hazard of his own
> life, as an image of himself, when he took Anchises on his shoulder, and
> bore him safe through the rage of the fire, and the opposition of his
> enemies; and therefore, *in the posture of a retiring man, who avoids the
> combat, he stretches out his arm in sign of peace, with his right foot
> drawn a little back, and his breast bending inward, more like an orator
> than a soldier.*

The amazing fact about the portion of Dryden's comment that I have
italicized is that Aeneas' elaborately described posture existed only
in the mind of Dryden the critic: it is present neither in Vergil's original nor Dryden's own translation. The only gesture that could have
suggested it is Aeneas' stretching forth his hand in pity to the youthful
warrior after the death blow had been delivered. Dryden has re-

sponded to Vergil's hint by imaginatively carving the hero into a statue in the antique manner. Nothing could be more characteristic of the motion of the neoclassical mind than that. It is constantly freezing the motions of nature and of antecedent literary art into the picturesque.

Dryden himself did exactly that in his own verse-adaptations. In his version of the "Knights Tale," which he entitled "Palamon and Arcite," he has elaborated upon Chaucer's description of the painting of Diana that hangs on the walls of her temple. Chaucer gave her only her silver bow and quiver and had her tread upon the crescent moon, her peculiar emblem. These details Dryden retains but dilates them into a fully developed iconic pose that resembles Correggio's and Rubens' famous Dianas, adding the details italicized in the following passage

> The graceful goddess was array'd in green;
> About her feet were little beagles seen,
> *That watch'd with upward eyes the motions of their queen.*
> *Her legs were buskin'd, and the left before*
> *In act to shoot;* a silver bow she bore,
> And at her back a *painted* quiver wore.
> She trod a wexing moon, that soon would wane,
> *And, drinking borrow'd light, be fill'd again.*
>
> (Book II, ii, 643-50)

What has happened to Chaucer is extremely revealing. Dryden has introduced metaphysical conceit and intellectual paraphrase. He has also added visual detail, stylized in a pictorial manner. The legs are buskined, and one of them, as in the imagined posture of Aeneas, is thrust forward in frozen action. The dogs look up to their queen. When we observe that exactly the same kind of ornamentation is added to Vergil and Chaucer by Pope and to Milton by Thomson and Collins, we must conclude that we here confront one of the dominant characteristics of neoclassical poetic expression.

It is not surprising, then, that it should be so important in Dryden's greatest play, the classically conceived *All for Love*. Some of its pictorial elements Dryden borrowed from his sources. The description of Cleopatra lying in her barge like "another sea-born Venus," surrounded by nymphs and fanned by boys who resemble cupids while the winds play about her face and lodge in the sails, is elaborately pictorial, but perhaps no more so than the magnificent passage in Shakespeare. In the final scenes, however, Dryden has intensified the pictorialism of his predecessors. In Plutarch, who liked pictorial effects even in prose history, the dead Cleopatra lies stretched out on a golden bed; Iras lies dead at her feet; Charmion, half-dead and about to fall, stands adjusting the queen's diadem. Samuel Daniel's setting is the

same, and one of the details is worked into the lovely line: "And dying
Charmion trimming of her head." In Shakespeare Charmion adjusts
the crown which is awry; and when the first guard asks "Where is the
Queen?" Charmion replies: "Speak softly, wake her not," words reminiscent of Michelangelo's famous lines on his statue Night. But Dryden's arrangement, though obviously indebted to his literary predecessors, is even more pictorial. Antony, dead on one throne, is placed
next to Cleopatra, who, though dead, sits erect on another. Charmion
stands behind her dressing her hair, and Iras, already dead, is stretched
out on the ground at her feet.[3]

All for Love and the "Choice of Hercules"

In placing *All for Love* alongside one of the most typical and
famous paintings of the seventeenth century I do not wish to argue a
conscious influence from canvas to play. Such influence is not at all
unlikely or uncommon; it can be widely illustrated in the period we
are studying. There is, however, no evidence for it in this instance;
had it existed, it seems probable that Dryden would have said something about it in the Preface he wrote for the drama. But I do wish,
in bringing *All for Love* and the "Choice of Hercules" together, to
support what I have been arguing, that the play is an example of the
neoclassical picturesque not only in certain of its details but in its
total impression.

What was sometimes called the "Choice of Hercules" and at other
times "Hercules at the Crossroads" [4] was a popular and influential
representation of a story now almost forgotten. During the seventeenth
and eighteenth centuries, however, this story was a kind of archetypal
icon. It originated in antiquity, when Socrates allegedly used it to
illustrate Hesiod's comment that the way of wickedness is easy and
degrading and the way of virtue hard and ennobling.[5] While passing
from boyhood to manhood, Hercules sat pondering in a quiet place
in the forest where two ways met. He was approached by two women
of great stature. The first was fair and tall, with modest eyes and a
figure soberly clad in white. The second was soft and plump from high
feeding, her face painted in an attempt to heighten its pink and white,
and her dress disclosing most of her charms. She habitually looked to

---

[3] These passages have been assembled by Bonamy Dobrée, *Restoration Tragedy*
(Oxford, 1929), pp. 80-1.

[4] The fortunes of this theme during the Renaissance have been traced in two
important studies: Erwin Panofsky, *Hercules am Scheidewege und andere antike
Bildstoffe in der neueren Kunst* (Leipzig-Berlin, 1930); Theodor E. Mommsen,
"Petrarch and the Story of the Choice of Hercules," *Journal of the Warburg and
Courtauld Institutes*, XVI (July-December, 1953), 178-92.

[5] Xenophon, *Memorabilia*, ii, 1. 21-33.

see whether anyone noticed her and stole glances at her own shadow. She told Hercules that she was called Happiness by her friends and Vice by her enemies, and she promised him all the joys of the flesh. The first woman, Virtue, summoned him to a high and noble road, but one that would cost him toil and effort. Choosing it, he would win renown as a hero and civilizer. There is no indication of which choice Hercules made, but his subsequent achievements witness that he chose the hard life of Virtue.

Of the long and varied fortunes of this legend we can here say little. Although told by Cicero and therefore known to the Middle Ages, it lay dormant through all the Christian centuries until Petrarch revived it, when it became one of the most popular themes of Renaissance Italy and Germany, giving to each of these countries a proverbial phrase "Ercole al Bivio," "Hercules am Scheidewege." The legend underwent changes in emphasis and served various purposes at various historical moments. We shall discuss only a few of the leading seventeenth- and eighteenth-century uses of this subject in order to indicate how deeply it had penetrated into the baroque culture that Dryden drew upon and into the neoclassical culture that he helped to create.

Annibale Carracci was one of the most influential painters of the *Seicento,* partly because he was sponsored by Bellori as reviver of the noble art and as an idealistic counterinfluence to the vulgar naturalism of Caravaggio and partly because he understood a culture that wished to retain the splendors of the Renaissance but also to interpret them afresh. Besides that, Annibale was a painter of considerable power whom literary people found attractive. His version of the Hercules was one of the most famous paintings of the epoch; knowledge of it was widely diffused, not only through copying and engraving, but through the long and eloquent description and analysis of it given by Bellori in his biography of Annibale.[6]

On Carracci's canvas which in the seventeenth and eighteenth centuries was hung in the Farnese Palace in Rome, where it could be

---

[6] Bellori's reading of this painting is highly literary, dramatic, and psychological. He actually puts words in the mouth of Virtue (*Vite* [Pisa, 1821], 36-39). In our own day Carracci's painting has been called by Mahon "a veritable masterpiece" and by Venturi an *opera mancata* (Denis Mahon, "Eclecticism and the Carracci," *Journal of the Warburg and Courtauld Institutes,* XVI [July-December, 1953], 340). Luigi Lanzi wrote at the end of the eighteenth century: "To write the history of the Carracci is equivalent to writing the history of painting of the last two centuries" (cited by R. Wittkower, *The Drawings of the Carracci* [London, 1952], p. 9). Almost all the English travelers were impressed by the works of the Carracci; of them, Annibale's works at the Farnese, including "Hercules at the Crossroads," impressed them the most. See Adolfo Venturi, *I Carracci e la loro scuola* (Milan, 1895) and Paolo Della Pergola, *I Carracci* (Rome, 1932).

admired along with the same artist's famous ceiling and his other moral allegories, Hercules appears as a young giant, nude, beardless, a frown of indecision on his face.[7] He stands in the center, almost equidistant from the two figures but slightly closer to Virtue, to whom he seems, though not decisively, to be inclining. Virtue faces the spectator, but her head is slightly turned toward Hercules. A modest creature, dressed in the robe and bearing the aegis of Athena, she points upward to a hill. By her side sits a bearded man, whose crown of laurel and open book reveal him to be an author who will celebrate Hercules' exploits if he chooses the proper path. To the right, her back to the spectator, stands the figure of sensuality, Voluptas, as she was usually called, clothed only in delicate and transparent stuff. She too looks at Hercules; her right arm, unlike that of Virtue, points downward. Two theatrical masks, an open songbook, and a musical instrument lie on the ground as the emblems of her blandishments.

Rubens also painted the theme. On his canvas, which is now at the Uffizi Gallery in Florence, the three characters are bound closely together by strong and restless rhythms of line and light. Voluptas, a Rubensian Venus if there ever was one, is almost nude. Two winged *amori* and two maidens, one of whom has flowers in her hair, support her pleas. Virtue is Amazonian. Wearing a helmet and a breastplate, she is in every way soldierly and strong. Instead of the poet of Annibale's scene, Rubens has drawn Time as a winged being in descent; his presence symbolizes the future renown that will follow the choice of Virtue. The military nature of Virtue's cause is emphasized by a youth who holds a bridled horse ready to bear Hercules away to his arduous exploits. In this painting Hercules seems inclined to Voluptas; not only is he facing her but the look on his face is one of yielding languor. Rubens' is a clear presentation of the conflict between hard military honor and soft sensuality.

These are the graphic representations most relevant to Dryden's play. Later uses of the theme we can only mention: the painting by Pompeo Battoni, which obviously influenced that of Paolo Matthaeis, whose somewhat simpler eighteenth-century version has most of the neoclassical features that the Earl of Shaftesbury instructed him to include; the parodies of the theme by Hogarth in the "March to Finchley" and by Reynolds in his spirited "Garrick between Comedy and Tragedy"; and its several appearances in literature from the Renaissance to the Romantic movement in the verses of Ariosto, Ben Jonson, Metastasio, Shenstone, Lowth, and Akenside, in the libretto of Handel's opera on the theme, and in Coleridge. Such manifestations of the theme should

---

[7] For reproductions of some of the paintings mentioned in this article see plates VI, VII A, VII B, VIII A and VIII B in *The Sister Arts.*

perhaps be intensively studied. They would reveal how deeply the
story had penetrated into neoclassical culture. It had become a uni-
versally accepted icon for difficult moral choice. Coleridge has his Laska
in *Zapolya* say:

> Well then! Here I stand,
> Like Hercules, on either side a goddess.
> Call this *(looking at the purse)*
> Preferment; this *(holding up the key)* Fidelity!
> And first my golden goddess: what bids she? [8]

A soldier hesitating between wife and mistress, an actor wavering
between the choice of tragedy or comedy, and a dramatic character
unable to decide between preferment and fidelity in his trust have all,
as these examples show, suggested the "Choice of Hercules" as symbol
and emblem. There would have been much greater reason for making
that story the emblem of Antony hesitating between Roman military
virtue and Egyptian love, for Antony had been prominently associated with Hercules in Dryden's leading sources. In Plutarch he is
presented as a descendant of Hercules, whom he resembled, a resemblance he sought "to confirme in all doings"—in dress, gait, bearing,
and speech.[9] The relationship with Hercules is even more strongly
suggested in Shakespeare. Cleopatra calls him "this Herculean Roman"
(Act I, Sc. 3), and Antony cries out

> The shirt of Nessus is upon me, teach me,
> Alcides, thou mine ancestor, thy rage (Act IV, Sc. 12).

When the second soldier, upon hearing the furtive and mysterious
music, says,

> 'Tis the god Hercules, whom Antony lov'd,
> Now leaves him (Act IV, Sc. 3),

[8] Act III, Sc. 1. Shaftesbury, "A Notion of the Historical Draught or Tablature
of the Judgment of Hercules," *Second Characters*, ed. Benjamin Rand (Cambridge,
Mass., 1914), pp. 360-61; Edgar Wind, "Borrowed Attitudes in Reynolds and Ho-
garth," *Journal of the Warburg and Courtauld Institutes*, II (1938-39), 182-85;
Ellis K. Waterhouse, *Painting in Britain: 1530 to 1790* (London, 1953), p. 168;
Orlando Furioso, vi, 55 ff; Metastasio, *Alcide al bivio;* Handel's interlude, "The
Choice of Hercules" (1750); Alfred Owen Aldridge, "The Eclecticism of Mark
Akenside's 'The Pleasures of the Imagination,'" *Journal of the History of Ideas*,
V (June, 1944), 312-13; "Pleasure reconcil'd to Vertue," *Ben Jonson*, ed. C. H. Her-
ford, Percy Simpson, and Evelyn Simpson, VII (Oxford, 1941), 483 ff. One of the
latest uses of the theme in painting is the central compartment of the "new" ceil-
ing, done earlier this century, by Lodovico Poliaghi for the Olympic Theater in
Vicenza.

[9] Shakespeare, *Antony and Cleopatra*, ed. M. R. Ridley ("Arden" ed. [London,
1954]), pp. 160, 258, 262, 280 (where the relevant passages from Plutarch are reprinted).

Shakespeare has substituted Hercules for Bacchus, who in Plutarch's account is believed to forsake Antony.

That association of Antony and Hercules Dryden maintained. On three separate occasions [10] Antony addresses prayers and ejaculations to his ancestor, and he is everywhere presented as a man of heroic and godlike proportions, even in his sufferings.

These associations, however, do not in themselves make the parallel with the painting valid. Such correspondence could not be legitimately applied to Shakespeare's *Antony and Cleopatra.* It is the total construction of *All for Love,* the arrangement of its characters, and the nature of their alternatives that are pictorial. In the enormous reduction of scenes and characters and in the severe condensation of time Dryden has approached the neoclassical picturesque—what he considered in his criticism the desirable economy of painting. Dryden's Antony—and this is not at all true of Shakespeare's—is, like Hercules, unmistakably at the center of the scene; Cleopatra, now somewhat reduced in scale and importance, is more or less on the level of Ventidius, who has been elevated in character and position until he can rival the queen herself; and both queen and soldier stand on either side of the hero, as it were, each urging the powerful and conflicting claims that lie at the center of Antony's choice. The entire machinery of the play operates to confront Antony with these two figures and the alternatives they represent. The first act is devoted to Antony and Ventidius and to the temporary triumph of Roman virtue. The second act is Cleopatra's triumph, as the first had been Ventidius'. And this type of alternating movement, though modified and complicated, continues through the drama. In its basic elements the choice of Antony is, then, the choice of Hercules: the dilemma of choosing between Ventidius, who represents military virtue, honor, friendship, and practical wisdom, and Cleopatra, who continues to represent, even in defeat and decline, the blandishments of love and the alluring pleasures of sense. [11]

In seeing this parallel we can also see how the author has transcended and enriched it. Dryden's Antony, an older man, cannot now

---

[10] Act II, Sc. 1 (twice); Act III, Sc. 1.

[11] Dryden continually makes us aware of the position of Ventidius and Cleopatra and of the nature of the conflict between them. When Ventidius first enters, Serapion says of him,

> "But, who's that stranger? By his warlike port,
> His fierce demeanour, and erected look,
> He's of no vulgar note" (Act I, Sc. 1).

Cleopatra's first words emphasize her conflict with Ventidius:

> "What shall I do, or whither shall I turn?
> Ventidius has o'ercome, and he will go . . ." (Act II, Sc. 1).

be made to encounter the clean-cut alternatives of a Hercules just entering manhood. In fact, Antony, a great soldier and a great lover, has chosen to travel both paths and has already achieved some of the glory of the one and some of the delight of the other. Though he does lose the world in death, it is "the world well lost."

Nor is Dryden's Cleopatra an exact equivalent of the Venus or the Voluptas of the painted legend. One should not deny her, as some have, all sensual allurement and make her another Octavia. But it is certainly true that Dryden's queen is something vastly different from and inferior to Shakespeare's. Capable of sorrow and sweetness, she has few feminine wiles. By no means the serpent of old Nile, she cannot act the role of duplicity that Alexas urges on her. The greatest mistress of all history wants nothing more than to be a wife:

> Nature meant me
> A wife; a silly, harmless, household dove,
> Fond without art, and kind without deceit (Act IV, Sc. 1).

Cleopatra's combination of sensual allure and the desire for uxorial virtue is foreign to the modern mind, and it has been judged very harshly. Churton Collins called her "wretched." Such judgment as this may spring in part from our complete insensitiveness to a type of womanhood greatly admired in the seventeenth century and often represented in baroque art. In such women, whether saint or sinner, there was a combination of sexual and religious ecstasy, of Ovidian voluptuousness and Christian sweetness. Precisely those qualities appear in Guido Reni's Cleopatra, who, about to apply the asps to her breast, looks heavenward, in an ecstatic gaze typical of Guido's saints, her mouth slightly open, her hair chastely tied up. She is a kind of Mary Magdalen, whom, in Guido's mind, she closely resembled.[12]

In closing the discussion of Dryden's play, I wish to repeat that I have not argued what is essentially unprovable, that Dryden borrowed directly from Annibale Carracci's canvas or one similar to it. It is true that in 1695 he knew the painting and Bellori's comment on it, for he described Annibale's "Farnesian gallery" as being morally instructive, "particularly the *Herculis Bivium,* which is a perfect triumph of virtue over vice; as it is wonderfully well described by the ingenious Bellori." [13] But strong though the likelihood is that this knowledge

---

[12] Collins' comment is quoted in Frederick Tupper and James W. Tupper, *Representative English Dramas* (New York, 1914), p. 42. J. Max Patrick, in a paper delivered at the Modern Language Association in 1955, said that the Cleopatra of Giraldi's *Cleopatra Tragedia* (1543) was the lamenting type, introduced in the sixteenth century as a neo-Senecan motif.

[13] *Works of Dryden,* ed. Walter Scott and George Saintsbury (London, 1892), XVII, 305.

was his when he was writing *All for Love,* it cannot at present be proved. What I have intended by the juxtaposition is to make clearer the fundamentally pictorial nature of the tragedy. Whether that quality came to Dryden's imagination directly from the canvases and frescoes of baroque and Bolognese art, from the dramatic pictorialism of the French classical theater, from the masque, or from the pictorialist tradition of the ancient poetry that he admired and translated is not important. *All for Love* is a manifestation of *ut pictura poesis,* a realization of Simonides' dictum that poetry should be a speaking picture. It is not a closely concatenated action that unfolds moral justice. It is a gallery of related heroic poses intended to arouse our sympathy (because the characters remain human beings and share our common nature) and our admiration (because they are larger than life, ideal forms in heroic postures). This play is substantive evidence of what Dryden meant when he said that the general parallel between poetry and painting is "more complete in tragedy" than in any other literary genre.

The Herculean Hero

by Eugene M. Waith

The comparison of *All for Love* with Shakespeare's *Antony and Cleopatra* has been an exercise for innumerable students, the subject of at least one German dissertation,[1] and of a few sentences in every history of the drama. Here, aside from an occasional reference to Shakespeare, the context will be Dryden's other plays. It is easy to exaggerate the differences between *All for Love* and the two heroic plays already discussed [*The Conquest of Granada* and *Aureng-Zebe*]. Dryden himself led the way towards putting it in a category apart not only by abandoning couplets to "imitate the divine Shakespeare," [2] but by his comment in the late essay, "A Parallel of Poetry and Painting," that he never wrote anything (presumably meaning any of his plays) for himself but *Antony and Cleopatra* (Ker, II, 152). Since Dryden's time critics have considered it exceptional in having an artistic merit which they deny to *The Conquest of Granada* or *Aureng-Zebe*, and one of the most astute of the recent critics has seen it as an exception in Dryden's thematic development.[3] There can be no doubt that there are differences, but the resemblances which bind *All for Love* to its predecessors, if less obvious, are very strong. The verse is certainly much freer; yet it retains often the antithetical balance common to heroic couplets, as when Cleopatra says of Caesar:

> He first possess'd my person; you, my love:
> Caesar lov'd me; but I lov'd Antony. (II 353-4)

Though emotion is presented with more immediacy in this play than in *The Conquest of Granada*, the basic concerns from which the emo-

From The Herculean Hero *(New York: Columbia University Press, 1962; London: Chatto & Windus, Ltd., 1962), by Eugene M. Waith, pp. 188-200. Copyright © 1962 by Eugene M. Waith. Reprinted by permission of the publishers.*

1 F. Hannmann, *Dryden's Tragödie "All for Love" und ihr Verhältnis zu Shakespeare's "Antony and Cleopatra"* (Rostock, 1903).

2 Preface to *All for Love. Essays of John Dryden*, ed. W. P. Ker (Oxford, Clarendon Press, 1926, two volumes), I, 200. All quotations from Dryden's critical writing are taken from this edition.

3 John Winterbottom, "The Development of the Hero in Dryden's Tragedies," *Journal of English and Germanic Philology*, 52 (1953), 162.

tions arise remain very similar, and the entire framework of feeling
and thought within which the characters discuss their problems is the
same. If the characters of *All for Love* are less stylized in presentation,
they are still of the same family as the characters in Dryden's other
heroic plays.

One of the family connections is seen in the traits of the Herculean
hero which reappear in Antony. Though the title of the play leaves no
doubt about the primacy of the theme of love, the hero, like his
prototype in Shakespeare's play, is a warrior whose nobility and generosity are combined with strong passion and a contemptuous disre-
gard for the mores of his society. Dryden's Antony manifests these
characteristics in ways which relate him even more closely to Almanzor
and Morat than to Shakespeare's hero. And Cleopatra is much more
closely related to other Dryden heroines than to Shakespeare's Cleopatra. These relationships must now be examined in more detail.

The first extended description of Antony is given by his general,
Ventidius, who is known to the Egyptians as one who does not share
in Antony's debauches, "but presides / O'er all his cooler hours" (I,
103-4):

> Virtue's his path; but sometimes 'tis too narrow
> For his vast soul; and then he starts out wide,
> And bounds into a vice, that bears him far
> From his first course, and plunges him in ills:
> But, when his danger makes him find his fault,
> Quick to observe, and full of sharp remorse,
> He censures eagerly his own misdeeds,
> Judging himself with malice to himself,
> And not forgiving what as man he did,
> Because his other parts are more than man. (I, 124-33)

Here again is an "irregular greatness" which cannot be quite contained within the bounds of virtue. Antony is farther than Almanzor
from being a "pattern of perfect virtue," much farther than Aureng-
Zebe, and not so far as Morat. The admiration of Ventidius is apparent, but equally so is his Roman attempt to distinguish neatly
between what is to be praised and blamed in Antony. As Aureng-Zebe
tries to dissect the paradox of Morat into man and brute, Ventidius
divides Antony into erring man and "more than man," but in spite
of this logical division the implication of the speech is that virtue and
vice are distinctions of secondary importance when discussing so vast
a soul. Later in the play, echoing the "taints and honours" speech of
Shakespeare's Maecenas, he says:

> And sure the gods, like me, are fond of him:
> His virtues lie so mingled with his crimes,

>   As would confound their choice to punish one,
>   And not reward the other. (III, 48-51)

The impossibility of confining Antony's spirit is the essence of his heroic individuality. When his fortune has ebbed to its lowest point, he compares his fortitude to a "native spring" which again fills the dried river-bed to overflowing:

>   I've still a heart that swells, in scorn of fate,
>   And lifts me to its banks. (III, 133-4)

The image recalls Shakespeare's Antony, but echoes Almanzor more closely:

>   I cannot breathe within this narrow space;
>   My heart's too big, and swells beyond the place. (I *Conquest*, V, 3, 23-4)

In Ventidius' initial description Antony's love is sharply differentiated from his virtue. It is obviously the vice into which the great man has "bounded"—an unruly, excessive infatuation. It may be compared with the "wild deluge" of the opening lines of the play, where Serapion is talking of "portents and prodigies." To stem this disastrous flow is the task which Ventidius has set himself, regardless of the admiration he has for Antony's largeness of spirit.

It is a commonplace of criticism that the first act of Dryden's play is dominated by Ventidius. Never again are we so completely in the warrior's world. From a dramatic point of view the showpiece of this act, and indeed one of the best scenes of the entire play, is the quarrel and reconciliation of Antony and his general. It has always been thought to derive from the famous quarrel and reconciliation of Brutus and Cassius, and Hart and Mohun, who took these parts in Shakespeare's play, distinguished themselves as Antony and Ventidius. Dryden preferred the scene, as he states in the preface, to anything he had written "in this kind." It bears a certain resemblance to the reconciliation of Aureng-Zebe with his father and more to the quarrel and reconciliation of Dorax and Don Sebastian, written many years later. In all of these scenes the generosity of the heroic mind triumphs over *amour propre*.

The significance of Antony's scene with Ventidius, however, is totally different from that of Aureng-Zebe's scene with the Emperor. Not only is the hero in this instance more sinning than sinned against, but the result of the dialogue is to arouse, not to pacify, the party at fault. The Emperor had to be induced to give up the senseless persecution of his son; Antony has to be roused from the torpor of remorse. Antony's change is presented in a highly dramatic contrast. At the beginning of the scene he throws himself on the ground, calling himself the "shadow of an emperor" and thinking of the time when he will be "shrunk to a few cold ashes." At the end, standing with Ventidius, he says:

> O, thou has fir'd me; my soul's up in arms,
> And mans each part about me. (I, 438-9)

The vital spark which makes him great has been restored.

In *All for Love* appears again the contrast between the fiery spirit and the cold one, analogous, as I have suggested, to Dryden's familiar contrast between wit and dullness. Though Antony is cold and torpid at the beginning, he is by nature fiery, and is brought to himself by the force of friendship. Caesar, his opposite, is "the coldest youth," who gives "so tame" an answer to Antony's challenge, has not even warmth enough to die by a fever, and rather than risk death will "crawl upon the utmost verge of life" (II, 113-30).

> O Hercules! Why should a man like this,
> Who dares not trust his fate for one great action,
> Be all the care of heav'n? (II, 131-3)

The task that Ventidius accomplishes in the first act may be looked at in two ways. It is in one sense a curbing and controlling of Antony. This aspect is suggested early by Ventidius' stern disapproval of Cleopatra's lavish plans for celebrating Antony's birthday. But it is also the firing of Antony's soul, and this is the aspect which is emphasized. To Ventidius the enemy is, of course, Cleopatra, but the worst of her effect on Antony is to have made him a "mute sacrifice" and "the blank of what he was." The state of mind which Ventidius has to combat directly is a paralysing remorse:

> You are too sensible already
> Of what y'have done, too conscious of your failings; (I, 312-13)

> you sleep away your hours
> In desperate sloth, miscall'd philosophy. (I, 336-7)

In fact Antony is at this time in a state very similar to Samson's when Manoa comes, in the second episode of *Samson Agonistes,* to warn him against being "over-just" with himself. The maintaining of the inner fire is so important a part of Dryden's concept of the heroic that it is stressed even in the depiction of Cleomenes, the nearly perfect hero of Dryden's last tragedy. The words of Cleomenes' mother might be almost as well applied to Antony:

> This melancholy flatters, but unmans you.
> What is it else, but penury of soul,

A lazy frost, a numbness of the mind,
That locks up all the vigour to attempt,
By barely crying,—'tis impossible! (I, Scott-Saintsbury, VIII, 276)

Only when Cleomenes assures her that his is a grief of fury, not despair, is his mother satisfied. "Desperate sloth," "penury of soul," "a lazy frost"—by the heroic code these are the true sins, beside which other forms of moral deviation pale.

Cleopatra is first seen as the cause of Antony's unmanning. The theatrical strategy of this first unfavorable impression, established only to be radically altered later on, is almost the only similarity between Dryden's treatment of his heroine and Shakespeare's. After exposure to the charms of Shakespeare's Cleopatra, who manages to remain marvellously attractive even at her most hoydenish and deceitful ("holy priests bless her when she is riggish"), one is apt to find the Cleopatra of Dryden shockingly tame and stiff. While it is easy to picture Shakespeare's Cleopatra in anything from Egyptian dress to the bodice and farthingale she probably wore on the Elizabethan stage, Dryden's Cleopatra belongs in late seventeenth-century court dress, complete with train. Passion never quite robs her of dignity. There is no haling of messengers by the hair, no riggishness. To understand this Cleopatra is an essential preliminary to understanding the play.

She dominates the second act as Ventidius does the first. In her initial appearance with Iras and her eunuch, Alexas, she proclaims her love a "noble madness" and a "transcendent passion" which has carried her "quite out of reason's view" till she is "lost above it" (II, 17-22). Force and excessiveness combine here with nobility as they do in Ventidius' first description of Antony. The heroine is no mere temptress to lure the hero from the path of virtue.[4] She is herself carried away by a passion of heroic proportions like his. Serapion's description of the flood, already suggested as an analogue for Antony's love, may be associated even more properly with Cleopatra's:

Our fruitful Nile
Flow'd ere the wonted season, with a torrent
So unexpected, and so wondrous fierce,
That the wild deluge overtook the haste
Ev'n of the hinds that watch'd it . . . (I, 2-6)

Dryden has taken over Shakespeare's insistence on the resemblances between the lovers and added another in giving Cleopatra a heroic

[4] Largely for this reason I cannot accept in its entirety the interesting parallel between the play and Carracci's "Choice of Hercules" proposed by Jean Hagstrum, *The Sister Arts* (Chicago: University of Chicago Press, 1958), p. 184 ff.

stature like Antony's. Grandeur and largeness of mind are hers as
much as they are his. In fact it is her high-mindedness rather than her
sensual attraction which persuades Antony not to leave her. The telling blow is her announcement that she refused a kingdom from Caesar
because of her loyalty to Antony (in her noble contempt for wealth
she resembles the Cleopatra of Fletcher and Massinger's *The False
One*). By the end of the act these similar lovers have been brought
together to the dismay of Ventidius, but it is to be noticed that Antony's conviction that Cleopatra is worth more than all the world
does not alter his heroic determination to fight with Caesar. There
is now the additional motive of revenge for Caesar's attempt to corrupt Cleopatra. Love for her is not entirely the effeminizing passion
Ventidius thinks it to be, and despite her dignified bearing she is far
from tame.

One sentence of self-description has exposed Cleopatra to a great
deal of unfriendly laughter:

> Nature meant me
> A wife; a silly, harmless, household dove,
> Fond without art, and kind without deceit. (IV, 91-3)

The comparison is not apt, and it is particularly unfortunate that the
incongruity blocks the understanding of a crucial point—Cleopatra's
attitude towards being a wife. In Shakespeare's play "Husband I
come" owes its brilliance as much to its unexpectedness as to its right-
ness. It signals a transformation in Cleopatra matching the re-emer-
gence of the heroic Antony. In Dryden's play the change is a much
smaller one, and so thoroughly prepared that it is no shock to hear:

> I have not lov'd a Roman, not to know
> What should become his wife; his wife, my Charmion!
> For 'tis to that high title I aspire . . . (V 412-14).

Her first reference to marriage is contemptuous, as one might expect.
Charmion has brought a message that, though Antony is leaving, he
will always respect Cleopatra, and she picks up the word with obvious
irritation:

> Is that a word
> For Antony to use to Cleopatra?
> O that faint word, *respect!* how I disdain it!
> Disdain myself, for loving after it!
> He should have kept that word for cold Octavia.
> Respect is for a wife: am I that thing,
> That dull, insipid lump, without desires,
> And without pow'r to give 'em? (II, 77-84)

The speech not only expresses Cleopatra's pique but establishes an attitude towards the cold and the dull exactly like that of Antony (the speech precedes Antony's comments on Caesar by only thirty lines). Though Cleopatra in other moods and other circumstances speaks more favourably of being a wife, she retains to the end her scorn of a "dull, insipid lump." Immediately after vowing to follow the dead Antony as a dutiful wife, she adds:

> Let dull Octavia
> Survive, to mourn him dead: my nobler fate
> Shall knit our spousals with a tie too strong
> For Roman laws to break. (V, 415-18)

The opposition between "spousals" and "Roman laws" provides the necessary clue here. Cleopatra considers her love above and beyond law as it is above and beyond reason, yet she borrows from marriage-law the terms which distinguish this love from an infatuation of the senses. Her unfortunate self-comparison to a household dove (the context of which will have to be examined later) is part of this process of distinguishing her feelings both from the dullness of the routine and every-day and from the purely sensual and transient.

A glance back at *The Conquest of Granada* will make the distinction clear. Cleopatra's love (and Antony's too) is the sort that Queen Isabella defines.[5]

> Love's a heroic passion which can find
> No room in any base degenerate mind:
> It kindles all the soul with honor's fire,
> To make the lover worthy his desire. (2 *Conquest,* I, 1, 145-8)

The fire and honor of such a love distinguish it from the "lethargy" to which Abdalla succumbs under Lyndaraxa's spell and also from the mere legality of Almahide's relationship to Boabdelin, "When all I knew of love, was to obey!" Almanzor at first takes love for a "lethargy," but by the time of his debate with Lyndaraxa he has learned that though it is not controlled by reason it is both constant and strong:

> 'Tis an enchantment where the reason's bound;
> But Paradise is in th'enchanted ground . . .
> My love's my soul; and that from fate is free;
> 'Tis that unchang'd and deathless part of me. (2 *Conquest,* III, 3, 146-7, 179-80)

Similarly, Antony is lethargic at the opening of the play, seemingly unmanned by love. He is "fired" first by Ventidius though still half

---

See Scott C. Osborn, "Heroical Love in Dryden's Heroic Drama," *Publications of the Modern Language Association,* 73 (1958), 480-90.

unwilling to leave Cleopatra. When she has persuaded him of the nobility of her love, he identifies his passion with his heroism, much as Almanzor does, and prepares with a whole heart for his battle with Caesar. The spectacle of triumph with which the third act opens presents the momentarily successful fusion of warrior and lover.

When Cleopatra compares herself to a household dove she is explaining to Alexas why she does not want to adopt his plan of flirting with Dolabella to arouse Antony's jealousy: she is opposed to all deceit. Repeatedly during the play her plainness is brought out. Though she finally takes the advice of Alexas, she is unable to maintain the counterfeit. Later, when the false news of her death is carried to Antony, she, unlike Shakespeare's heroine, is unaware of the ruse. Antony, too, has a transparent nature, and both of them in this respect resemble Almanzor, who compares his heart to a crystal brook. Antony complains of his "plain, honest heart," and compares himself to "a shallow-forded stream" (IV, 432-40). Plainness is another heroic trait which Dryden has given to Cleopatra; his desire to emphasize it in the scene with Dolabella leads him to force the comparison of his heroine to a wife, who is further compared to a fond and artless dove. If Cleopatra lacks the dullness of a wife, she hopes to prove that she lacks the meretriciousness of a mistress.

The comparison of two kinds of love is best seen in Cleopatra's interview with Antony's legal wife, who is hardly more like a household dove than Cleopatra. Dryden was well aware that the unhistorical introduction of Octavia in Act III was his most daring innovation. I doubt whether it has the effect which Dryden most feared, of dividing the audience's sympathies (and he notes that no critic made this objection), but it has other consequences, very likely unintentional, though by no means damaging to the total effect of the play. Briefly stated, they are the shift from the contrast between Cleopatra and Caesar to the contrast between Cleopatra and Octavia and the resulting transfer of heroic values to the realm of love.

In Shakespeare's play Caesar remains throughout the chief embodiment of the Roman point of view as Cleopatra of the Egyptian. Caesar's ideal of heroic man is a Stoic concept of the warrior, whereas Cleopatra's includes both warrior and lover. The same might be said of the ideals of these two characters in *All for Love*, but from the moment that Octavia appears, she usurps her brother's antipodal position. The confrontation with Cleopatra establishes her firmly as Antony's alternative choice. Even Ventidius, who represents Roman values though qualified by his admiration for Antony, relies on Octavia to make the Roman ideal compelling. Thus, though the issue remains Antony's choice of love or his responsibilities in the world, the stage presents as the dramatic symbols of these alternatives two

women, Cleopatra and Octavia, and the choice at the center of the
play becomes one between love and marriage. The turn of the third
act which determines Antony for the second time to leave Cleopatra
is not, as it was in the first act, the responsibility to fight Caesar in
order to show the world who is master, but duty to a wife, through
whom he may reach a peaceful understanding with Caesar. Octavia's
weapons are her unrequited love and her children. Cleopatra, who
was portrayed in the first act as a deterrent to heroic action, now
appears as an alternative to domestic love. When the two women
meet, they naturally quarrel over which one of them loves Antony
more, and Cleopatra stakes her claim on the very extravagance of her
love, which has made her give up her good name in order to become
Antony's mistress. The fourth act in effect tests the truth of this love
in the episode of Dolabella, showing that it is too great to be con-
cealed. Octavia's love, in this same act, is overwhelmed by outrage.
When she leaves in the midst of angry (though justifiable) accusations,
it is reduced to duty, its basic component all along.

In the fifth act Antony is separated from both women. Octavia has
left and he has quarrelled with Cleopatra over her supposed liking
for Dolabella. The problems of empire are raised again but only to
be reabsorbed in the problems of love. Though the Egyptian fleet has
deserted and Caesar is at the gates, Antony is primarily concerned
with Cleopatra's feelings towards him. When he thinks that she has
fled, his first thought is that she has "fled to her Dolabella"; the
accusation that she has turned to Caesar comes second. The idea of a
heroic last stand is banished in an instant by the false news of Cleopatra's death, which seems to prove her innocence. The only possible
heroic action now is suicide, since

> I was but great for her; my pow'r, my empire,
> Were but my merchandise to buy her love . . . (V, 270-1)

The structure of the play has been called episodic. Noyes says that
"like that of *The Conquest of Granada*, it deals with successive adventures in the life of one man, not with one central crisis." [6] Jean
Hagstrum says the play "is not a closely concatenated action that unfolds moral justice. It is a gallery of related heroic poses intended to
arouse our sympathy . . . and our admiration . . ." (*The Sister Arts*,
p. 196). The second judgment is much the more acceptable, and surely
the relatedness which Hagstrum recognizes is provided by the crisis
in the love-relationship of Antony and Cleopatra, the concern of each
act in the play. It is strange to complain of looseness of structure in a

---

[6] *Selected Dramas of John Dryden*, ed. G. R. Noyes (Chicago: Scott, Foresman,
1910), p. xlix.

play whose strength resides in concentration upon one problem. In this respect the structure is a refinement upon that of *The Conquest of Granada* and *Aureng-Zebe*. The three plays constitute a series in progressive tightness and simplification.

In *All for Love* the Herculean hero's quest for unbounded power is replaced by a quest for unbounded love. In *The Conquest of Granada* a noble love modifies the masculine drive for power, redirecting it towards a goal acceptable to society. In *Aureng-Zebe* Indamora tries to exert a similar modifying and redirecting influence, but without achieving the same results as Almahide. Aureng-Zebe's love for her is his one unruly passion, and Morat gives up his ambition for "unjust dominion" only to replace it by a love which ignores marital bonds. We never see Antony, as we do Almanzor and Morat, at a time when military conquest is his chief aim. In spite of the efforts of Ventidius, the problems of empire rapidly sink to a position of secondary importance, hardly competing in Antony's mind with his desire for Cleopatra. At the end of the play, instead of the heroic image of him conjured up by Shakespeare's Cleopatra, we are presented with a stage picture of the bodies of the two lovers, regally attired and seated next each other in throne-like chairs. When Serapion finds them he says:

> See, see how the lovers sit in state together,
> As they were giving laws to half mankind! (V, 507-9)

Only in this paradoxical image is the idea of world-conquest restated, and even here it is subordinated to the triumph of love.

It is a curious fact that this play, which is so thoroughly a love-tragedy, is in one important respect closer to the pattern of Herculean plays than either *The Conquest of Granada* or *Aureng-Zebe*. In both of these plays the final emphasis is on a reconciliation of heroic energies with the laws of society. Almanzor remains an invincible hero but in the service of Ferdinand and Isabella. Morat's case is more ambiguous, but at the end death has removed his irregular greatness, and the compelling image of the hero lying at Indamora's feet gives way to tableaux of orderly family relationships. Aureng-Zebe, after a quarrel, is reconciled to Indamora. Melesinda marches in a religious procession to her husband's funeral pyre, where she will commit suttee. Nourmahal, the spirit of restless disorder, dies on the stage. Aureng-Zebe, having succeeded in restoring his father to power, receives the crown from his hands. In *All for Love* the effort to tame or redirect the hero's energies is totally unsuccessful. The love which the play celebrates soars beyond reason and legality, leading the lovers to defiance of the world and a final self-assertion in suicide. In his unrepentant commitment to a highly individualistic ideal, Antony is a logical successor to Morat, but far more Herculean that Almanzor or Aureng-Zebe.

For different reasons, the play as a whole is more like the other Herculean plays than is Shakespeare's *Antony and Cleopatra*. There Antony's love is more clearly an alternative to heroic action, however attractively that alternative is presented. In *All for Love* it is not merely that the world is well lost for such a love, but that Dryden, largely through his treatment of Cleopatra, has elevated the love and made its truth and strength unquestionable, though to attain it the world must be defied. Thus presented, it becomes a suitable enterprise for a hero.

In the preface Dryden makes it clear that the lovers are to be blamed for not controlling their passions and finds the attraction of the story in the "excellency of the moral," but he also states that he has drawn the characters of the hero and the heroine as favorably as his sources would permit him. His emphasis on the greatness and nobility of their love is obviously part of this process. The result is a powerful claim on the sympathy of the audience and perhaps less moral instruction than Dryden liked to think. In fact, the love of Antony and Cleopatra, elevated to the level of a "heroic passion," contains the very sort of contradictions which make a moral judgment of Tamburlaine or Bussy so difficult. The love itself is an extravagant, fiery force, knowing no obligations, and yet ennobling in spite of its extra-legality. It is a pattern of loyal commitment. One might say that the moral is not (as Dryden implies) the punishment of lovers who fail to control their passions, but the tragic limitations imposed by human existence on the infinite aspirations of heroic passion.

Passion and Pity in *All for Love*

by Otto Reinert

In many respects *All for Love* may be said to be faithful to the letter of the law governing life in the heroic play, but it certainly violates its spirit. The purpose of the heroic play, said Dryden in his essay on the genre (Preface to *The Conquest of Granada*), is 'to be an imitation, in little, of an heroic poem; and consequently, . . . Love and Valour ought to be the subject of it.'[1] Its end, like that of its revered prototype, was to imitate 'The highest pattern of human life' (Ker, I, 154), 'to raise admiration,' as Hobbes put it.[2] But in *All for Love*, compassion with romantic feeling in distress, not admiration for virtuous love and heroic valor, is the audience emotion courted. This was quite deliberate with Dryden. The one fault he admits to in the play is the tactical one of introducing Octavia as an object of pity:

> . . . the compassion she moved to herself and children was destructive to that which I reserved for Antony and Cleopatra; whose mutual love being founded upon vice, must lessen the favour of the audience to them, when virtue and innocence were oppressed by it. (Ker, I, 192)

And his comment on the play in the essay on the 'Parallel of Poetry and Painting' (1695) points to the same intention. There are, he says, three ways in which a poet can draw the character of his hero: panegyrically, neutrally, and pejoratively. In his adaptation of *Oedipus Rex* he had tried to imitate Sophocles' own panegyrical way,

> [but] my characters of Antony and Cleopatra, though they are favourable to them, have nothing of outrageous panegyric. Their passions were their own, and such as were given them by history; only the deformities of them were cast into shadows, that they might be objects of compas-

"Passion and Pity in All for Love*" by Otto Reinert. Abridged from* The Hidden Sense, *ed. Kristian Smidt (Oslo: Universitetsforlaget, 1963; New York: Humanities Press, Inc., 1963), pp. 176-95. Copyright © 1963 by Universitetsforlaget and Humanities Press, Inc. Reprinted by permission of the author and the publishers.*

[1] *Essays of John Dryden*, ed. W. P. Ker (Oxford, 1926), I, 150. Hereafter referred to as 'Ker.' Subsequent references will be given in the text.

[2] 'The Virtues of an Heroic Poem,' (Preface to translation of Homer's *Odyssey*, 1675), Spingarn, II, 68.

sion: whereas if I had chosen a noonday light for them, somewhat must
have been discovered which would rather have moved our hatred than
our pity. (Ker, II, 146)

In other words, Dryden did not scruple to reconcile the neoclassical
didactic function of literature with the painting of vice and unreason
in the colors of compassion.

Such a statement of intention is relevant to critical analysis only if
it accurately generalizes the actual specifics of the play. Dryden's here
does. Ventidius' first exclamation at the sight of the distraught emperor is, " 'Tis mournful, wondrous mournful!" [3] Alexas speaks of
Cleopatra's 'weak passion' (p. 360), Cleopatra of Antony's 'tender
heart' (p. 361), Charmion offers Antony the queen's 'pitiful request'
(p. 362), Alexas appeals to his 'soft pity' (p. 366), Antony says of himself that he has been 'Bred in the rules of soft humanity' (p. 369). It is
the news of Antony's failure to pity her plight (a false report, needless
to say) that breaks down Cleopatra's pose of gay flirtation with Dolabella. Even rugged Ventidius weeps more than once and feels pity for
Dolabella when he thinks him ensnared by Cleopatra (p. 404). The
dialogue of every major scene is full of words like 'soft,' 'tender,' 'fond,'
'gentle,' and 'mild,' the characters are forever pleading, sighing, 'melt-
ing,' and shedding tears, the action moves forward by an almost un-
broken sequence of emotional appeals and responses, with pity as the
main theme. The following is a typical exchange:

> *Octav* . . .
> Who made his children orphans, and poor me
> A wretched widow? only Cleopatra.
> *Cleo.* Yet she, who loves him best, is Cleopatra.
> If you have suffered, I have suffered more.
> You bear the specious title of a wife,
> To gild your cause, and draw the pitying world
> To favour it: the world condemns poor me; (Act III, p. 394)

This, like so many of the play's scenes of argument, concludes with a
display of emotion. The scenes in Act II (pp. 372-73) in which Cleopatra declines to defend herself against Antony's charge that she has
ruined him, not because she chooses not to stoop to self-justification
but because she will not admit reasoned and documented accusations
to a lovers' relationship—'Though I deserved this usage, Was it like
you to give it?'—is more than just another example of the general
pattern. It movingly and lucidly juxtaposes the play's two central,

[3] *The Dramatic Works of John Dryden,* ed. Sir Walter Scott and George Saintsbury (Edinburgh, 1882), V, 350. Subsequent references will be by page number only
and given in the text.

antithetical values. Dolabella's words to Antony, that 'pity must prevail' (p. 413), could stand as motto for the whole play. One recalls Dryden's reason (in the Prologue to *Aureng-Zebe,* p. 201) for being tired of rhyme: 'Passion's too fierce to be in fetters bound.' In the light of *All for Love* the line appears prophetic.[4]

But if *All for Love* is a tragedy of pity and pathos rather than of terror and admiration, its failure to raise a warning finger on the behalf of reason and sexual morality ceases to be a symptom of Dryden's confusion of thought or of his divided intent. If the play is to be reduced to a moral at all, it must be one of some such order as this: the lovers perish as all those must who stake their all on passion rather than on reason. But their fall effects a purgation of the emotion of pity in the audience, and this effect is achieved precisely because Dryden abandons the simple moral scheme of the heroic play for the complex, multiple truth of mature tragedy. The play points beyond the strict neoclassical mode also in its particularity. Dryden's achievement is that he succeeds, despite the rigor of his form and the low temperature of his language, in making us feel that for *these* lovers, in *these* circumstances, the world is well lost. I have already maintained that there is in principle no reason why the Preface to *All for Love* should be either a means of determining the paraphrasable thought content of the play itself or a norm for judging it; but if it is so used one finds, in fact, no inconsistency between, on the one hand, saying, as Dryden does in the Preface, that the 'greater height' of tragedy was inaccessible to him by the very facts of the legend, for the lovers' downfall was 'not occasioned by any necessity, or fatal ignorance, but [was] wholly voluntary; since our passions are, or ought to be, within our power' (Ker, I, 191-92), and, on the other hand, evoking pity and even a sense of waste that so great a power to love should be wrecked on undisciplined passion, that the order of the workaday world cannot accommodate such intensity of feeling. The lovers are not guiltless, but their guilt fulfils itself tragically. Love here is a consuming fire, but, like other victims of consuming tragic passions (Medea, Othello, Phèdre), the lovers are grand in their ashes. Dryden's rhetoric of sentiment and pity may be inadequate to full expression of his tragic theme, but his theme has been tragically conceived. *All*

4 Baxter Hathaway in 'John Dryden and the Function of Tragedy,' *PMLA,* LVIII (1943), 665-73, sees *All for Love* as a precursor of the sentimental drama of the eighteenth century. According to Hathaway, the older, Neo-Stoical tragedy of the seventeenth century sought catharsis through fear in the spectator, 'lest the passion overcome his reasoning faculty,' while the sentimentalists sought catharsis by means of tragic pity. Dryden 'stood at the crossroads between the two conceptions' (pp. 665-66). Hathaway's view seems to me to be sound. I should only argue that Dryden's alteration of Shakespeare's lovers shows him already started down the road to Sentiment.

for Love is a more complex play than it has generally been given credit for being.

The charge of disunity of plot focuses on the figure of Alexas and his role as intriguer in Acts IV and V. The difficulty is not, as one critic claims, that a 'major weakness' of Dryden's play in comparison with Shakespeare's, 'results from his alteration of the role of Alexas [who is little more than a supernumerary in Shakespeare], Cleopatra's facile pander,' with the result that 'the admirable self-sufficiency of Shakespeare's queen is considerably impaired.'⁵ The comment proves only the critic's failure to realize Dryden's altered intention with the story. That Dryden's queen is not only different from Shakespeare's but also a smaller, less fascinating, even, if one likes, a less fully realized piece of dramatic characterization, may be readily admitted. But that he simply blundered in softening Cleopatra's character or that his Cleopatra does not more intimately belong in the emotional climate of his play than Shakespeare's grand 'Egypt' would have done —is simply not true. The comment that Alexas serves as plot expedient by absorbing some of the odium that would otherwise attach to Cleopatra seems more to the point.⁶

But the main defect in Dryden's conduct of plot is his need for a character like Alexas at all. The intrigue element in Act IV and the early part of Act V is alien to the dominant mode of the play both before and after. Miss Wallerstein has put it cogently:

> [Dryden] created a circumstantial unity which could have had dramatic development only if Alexas had been a principal character; since that development was not present, he created in reality a second plot which is never more than an artificial husk around the essential drama of Antony and Cleopatra, though it does solve his difficulty in the motivation of Cleopatra.⁷

And one sees what Sale has in mind when he finds in Alexas' plot function a residue of the cruder dramaturgy of the heroic play:

> . . . it is [Alexas'] celerity in machination, as much as the regular reversal in each Act, turn and turn about, that enforces the similarity with the scene-by-scene palace revolutions and realignments which make the strict Heroic Play so fevered and difficult to follow.⁸

⁵ T. P. Harrison, '*Othello* as a Model for Dryden's *All for Love*,' Univ. of Texas *Studies in English*, no. 7 (1929), p. 136.

⁶ Norman Suckling, 'Dryden in Egypt, Reflexions on *All for Love*,' *Durham University Journal*, XLV (1952), 3-4.

⁷ Ruth Wallerstein, 'Dryden and the Analysis of Shakespeare's Techniques,' *Review of English Studies*, XIX (1943), 170.

⁸ Arthur Sale, ed. *All for Love*, 2nd edition (London, 1961), p. xix.

Compared with the first three acts, in which the successive pulls on Antony's loyalties are executed unilinearly and in a slow and stately measure, the intrigue phase of the action is fast-paced, fussily crowded and complicated, difficult to reconstruct in the memory. Scheming and suspense provide the motor force of the action, suspending, for a time, the subtle, double emotional movement in Antony, which is the play's inner action. For Antony vacillates not just between love and empire-honor-duty; he also moves vertically on a scale representing something one may call 'pitch of being,' the extremes of which are exaltation—whether of love, as at the end of Acts II and V; or of honor, love's antithesis in this connection, as at the end of Acts I and III—and lethargic dejection, as at the beginning of Acts I and V and the end of Act IV. For the duration of the intriguery this second movement depends on it since the intrigue carries it, but it is also obscured by the intrigue. And because the movement amounts to dramatic demonstration of the fact that emotional disengagement equals dull gloom in Antony and thus supports the play's general celebration of passion at reason's expense, and because it develops concurrently with the more obvious movement of Antony's see-sawing loyalties, and, by intersecting it, lends dynamic tension to the inner action, its interruption by the intrigue plot impedes and imperils the play's essential progress.

But this is the extent of the failure. If the jealousy intrigue and the false report of Cleopatra's death temporarily usurp primary dramatic interest and distract from the basic scenic image of feelings in flux, it is not irrelevant to the theme of the play. In fact, it vitally contributes to it. For the consequences of the intrigue which Alexas directs on the Egyptian side and which Ventidius, though ignorant of Alexas' schemes, yet furthers on the Roman side are evidence of the inadequacy of reason. Alexas' and Ventidius' plans both miscarry because both depend on rationality: they presume to predict Antony's psychological reactions. They fail, not because they do not accurately predict what emotions will ensue, but because they underestimate their strength. Antony's jealousy gets out of hand, and Act IV ends in general discomfiture. Alexas has not only failed to reconcile Antony and Cleopatra, he has deepened their alienation. Ventidius has not only not eradicated Cleopatra from Antony's heart, but has provoked him to reveal his love for her in such a manner as to drive Octavia away and thus preclude any honorable reconciliation with her brother Octavius. Dolabella, far from winning Cleopatra's love, has been the instrument of her grief and made himself miserable with the consciousness that he has betrayed Antony's friendship. As for the lovers themselves, Antony has lost empire, wife, children, friends, and love, while Cleopatra, desperate from her estrangement from Antony, attempts suicide. Feelings rampant have shattered reason's careful plans. At the end of Act IV, Antony, Cleopatra, and Dolabella have all demonstrated that they are not masters of their own psyche. Clearly, man is not manipulable, and this, I submit, is a thesis with which the whole play is centrally concerned.

If *All for Love* can be vindicated against charges of disunity of theme and at least partly against similar charges against its plot, a defense of its imagery can only modify, not refute, such censure. As recent studies of Shakespearean imagery, both purely verbal and in what Alan Downer calls 'the language of action,' [9] have revealed the inner unity of even as apparently diffuse a play as *Antony and Cleopatra*, a similar approach to *All for Love* has only disclosed a degree of chaos beneath the surface unity. The charge is Kenneth Muir's:

> There are rather more than two hundred images in *All for Love*, but there is no evidence that Dryden employs what Miss Spurgeon calls 'iterative imagery' . . . On the surface it appears that *All for Love* has greater unity than *Antony and Cleopatra;* but a study of the style, and particularly of the imagery of the two plays serves to show that Shakespeare's unity is deeper and more real than Dryden's, for it is a unity based on the poetic conception and expressed in a style, which, because it regards nothing as common or unclean, is never led into bathos or bombast. Dryden's style is sometimes sublime, but it is more frequently rhetorical, sometimes bombastic, and occasionally flat . . . His images do not spring naturally from his theme, as the leaves from a tree; they are improvised: and though they may illuminate separate ideas, feelings, and even characters and scenes, they serve to destroy rather than to create the unity of the whole. *All for Love* is a fine tragedy decorated with poetry. It is not a poetic tragedy in the truest meaning of the term.[10]

This is excellent and important criticism, only too easily supported. In the space of some 150 lines near the beginning of Act III (pp. 379-84) Antony appears, in succession, as the son of Hercules, as a lion, as riveted to Dolabella, as one of two confluent rivers, as an impatient bridegroom, as Dolabella's home, as a depleted river or dam, as the sun, as the goal of foot-racers, and as a dried-up tree. But this, after all, is only miscellaneousness, and if one is not consciously looking for patterns (and an audience hardly is) one is not likely to notice the imagistic disorder. And most of these images do adequately illus-

[9] 'The Life of Our Design: The Function of Imagery in Poetic Drama,' in *Shakespeare: Modern Essays in Criticism*, ed. Leonard F. Dean (New York, 1957), pp. 19-36.
[10] 'The Imagery of *All for Love*,' *Proceedings of the Leeds Philosophical and Literary Society*, V (1940), 140, 147.

trate their local contexts, in the manner Muir mentions. More vulnerable is the constellation of disparate images applied to Octavius (pp. 364-65): 'the minion of blind chance' is followed almost immediately by 'the coldest youth' who 'has not warmth enough to die by' fever, and that, in turn, by a flickering 'lamp' and a 'wren.' If these are not quite mutually contradictory images, their collaboration strains awkwardly and meaninglessly. And when Antony's pitying reluctance to bid Cleopatra goodbye prompts Dolabella's celebrated

> Men are but children of a larger growth;
> Our appetite as apt to change as theirs,
> And full as craving too, and full as vain; (pp. 396-97)

which anticipates later appearances of Antony as 'infant,' one uneasily reflects that one of the main appellations for Octavius, Antony's unemotional, unwavering foil, is 'boy.' Concise syntax and functional patterns of alliteration and assonance (particularly the witty near-pun of 'appetite as apt') cannot make up for the tectonic damage done to the theme by such casualness. Nor is this the only occasion on which the two emperors share imagery. Octavius is also a cold-blooded trader, a base weigher of gains and losses, a 'usurer: . . . fit indeed to buy, not conquer kingdoms' (p. 385). It is disconcerting, then, to find five images, one in Act III and four in Act V, that associate Antony too with the world of trade and finance. He speaks of himself as 'a thriftless debtor' to Octavia's and his daughters' loves (p. 390). Serapion calls him 'a bankrupt prodigal' (p. 421). Antony accepts each Roman life lost in his cause as his 'just debt' (p. 424), and sees himself as a 'merchant' (p. 425) and all his power as 'but merchandise to buy' Cleopatra's love (p. 427). The contrast between the successful and the unsuccessful merchant cannot cover up the consequent indistinctness of characterization or the basic inappropriateness of applying such images at all to the least mercenary of men as he is about to die for love. Antithetical characters share even more major imagery. When Antony's excessive emotionalism time and again is expressed in images of deficient manhood, the fact that Alexas, reason's representative, is a eunuch, a 'half-man' (p. 410), becomes a paradox close to opacity. Other examples of random and inconsistent imagery could be given. It is at best pointless to refer to both Cleopatra and Octavia as 'poison' for Antony (pp. 368, 386) and possibly worse than pointless for both Octavius and Cleopatra to appear as 'crocodile' (pp. 351, 366). Even in a deliberate lie it is faintly absurd to find Cleopatra, of all people, compared to the dying Lucrece (p. 426). But it is in the very nature of the thing that further illustration would be both depressing and useless. Perhaps the greatest harm done by the failure of such images to function cumulatively and consistently—or even always organically in the local passage—is that they get in the way of perception of images that *do* work in clusters and *are* pertinent to the dramatic whole, and—worse yet—that they raise disturbing queries whether such pertinent clusters exist outside the critic's over-eager mind.

Such critical self-doubts, I believe, can be silenced by reference to other parts of the play. My disagreement with Muir is one of degree only, but the degree is not inconsiderable. There is more than incidental support in the play for modification of Muir's statement that 'there is no evidence . . . of "iterative imagery" ' in *All for Love.*

Dryden prided himself on his action being 'so much one, that it is the only of the kind without episode, or underplot; every scene in the tragedy conducing to the main design, and every act concluding with a turn of it' (Ker, I, 192). It could perhaps be argued that the successive 'turns' represent episodes of a kind, and that Dolabella's dilemma in Act IV represents a parallel variant of Antony's and hence could be called a kind of small subplot, but Dryden's essential claim, that he had built a unified plot, can hardly be denied. In fact, he might have claimed more for his conduct of plot. His hero, as he recognized himself (Ker, I, 191), is clearly Aristotle's good man flawed, and manifestly the shape of the action reflects the central psychological fact about Antony: the double fluctuation between love and empire-honor-duty and between invigorating exaltation, whether as lover or as emperor-soldier-husband-father; and dejected lethargy, when he is emotionally uncommitted, is the plot equivalent, the embodiment in a comprehensive and ordering image of action, of the theme of Passion-versus-Reason. The recurrent plot event is Antony's changing his mind—or, since the idiom in this case is misleading, his emotional allegiance, and the plot is the function of its main motivating force: a man who, by his own statement in Act I, has lost his reason (p. 354). Every turn of the action—that is, every act conclusion—is brought about by some over-whelming rush of feeling, never by deliberate thought. At the end of Act I Ventidius arouses Antony from his Orsino-like revery not by the news of the twelve legions awaiting his command but by provoking first his anger and then remorse for that anger by his diatribe against Cleopatra as the cause of Antony's ruin. The turn in Act II comes when Cleopatra's rejection of Octavius' proffered bribe instantly annuls Antony's carefully argued bill of complaints against her. In Act III the turn is a spontaneous ritual of kind affection, a veritable climax of emotionalism:

> *Vent.* Was ever sight so moving?—Emperor!
> *Dola.* Friend!
> *Octav.* Husband!
> *Both Child.* Father!

        Ant. I am vanquished: take me,
    Octavia; take me, children; share me all.
                      [Embracing them.] (p. 390)

Act IV turns with the sudden revival of Antony's jealousy, his suspicion that Dolabella has taken his place in Cleopatra's affections. His suicide in Act V is caused by his grief and remorse at the (false) report of Cleopatra's death, and the emotional nature of his act is underscored by the fact that he bungles it: 'I've missed my heart' (p. 430).[11]

His words suggest a symbolic significance—as if the soldier cannot yet kill the lover; Love's finest moments are still to be lived. Rising above the 'desperate sloth, miscalled philosophy,' which was Ventidius' term for Antony's suicidal mood in Act I (p. 355), and which, in the form of a kind of pseudo-stoical Pyrrhonism, inspires his Hamlet-like temper at the moment of his actual suicide attempt here in Act V ('Books had spoiled him; For all the learned are cowards by profession. 'Tis not worth My further thought; for death, for ought I know, Is but to think no more. Here's to be satisfied'), Antony dies in Cleopatra's arms, happy at that exalted and intense pitch of being at which he fulfils his hyper-sensitive, mobile nature.

Throughout *All for Love* Love and the World are antithetical values—Antony's first reported speech, 'Take all, The world's not worth my care' (p. 347), through his 'Give to your boy, your Caesar, This rattle of a globe to play withal' (p. 376), and to his dying 'This one kiss—more worth Than all I leave to Caesar' (p. 432). The world is a world of reason, not just because an Octavius rules it, but also because Love repeatedly is presented as a form of madness. '[I] love out of reason's view,' says Cleopatra (p. 361), and 'my love's a noble madness,' and 'the foolish world, Which knows not tenderness, will think me mad' (pp. 361, 376). In Act I Antony calls himself 'madman' and 'fool' for having loved the world away (p. 354). The 'fool within' him

---

11 Cf. Mildred E. Hartsock ['Dryden's Plays: A Study in Ideas,' *Seventeenth Century Studies*, 2nd series, ed. Robert Shafer (Princeton, 1937), pp. 71-176]: 'Dryden's conversion to Hobbist psychology is further evidenced by a recurrent theme of inconstancy and vacillation' (p. 99) and 'The dramatist [Dryden] pictures a world dedicated to a naturalistic pursuit of passional ends; and the dwellers therein . . . , even when . . . they are designed to be heroic, . . . are still slaves to their emotions and self-centred ambitions' (p. 127). But Miss Hartsock refers to *All for Love* only once and then only briefly [Antony exemplifies 'the man of passion,' (p. 125)]. One can see why. Though their emotionalism, particularly Antony's instability, may be said to illustrate a critique of rationalism akin to Hobbes's, their selflessness vis-à-vis one another and the relatively slight importance of mere eroticism in their motivation limit the usefulness of Dryden's Antony and Cleopatra as supports of Miss Hartsock's thesis that ideologically Dryden's plays are indebted to Hobbes's materialistic determinism. The lovers hardly belong in any part of the libertine tradition.

tempts him to forgive Cleopatra in Act IV (p. 416). Alexas says that love deludes the sight while reason sees straight (p. 363). Dolabella calls loving 'mere madness all' (p. 397) and says of Cleopatra that she loves Antony 'to madness' (p. 413).

A related complex of images is that according to which man, lost to passion, becomes something other than or less than man. The concept is of course traditional in Christian humanism. Man's distinctive, God-given faculty is, precisely, his reason, and to abdicate from rationality is to leave one's God-appointed place in the scheme of things, to renounce one's part as man in the cosmic drama. Characteristically, the concept provides major and structural imagery in two such central works of English neoclassicism as the *Essay on Man* [12] and *Gulliver's Travels*.

Although not all the images in Act I that refer to Antony participate in this pattern (a disturbing handful includes 'god-like,' 'hero,' and 'meteor of the world'), a sufficient number is active in the theme of man *manqué* to refute Muir's stricture as it pertains to this part of the play. Antony appears as animal: his heart 'a prey to black despair' (p. 345), his soul an uncurbed horse (p. 347), himself a sacrificial lamb (p. 349), and a scorpion (p. 354); as an uprooted tree (p. 351); as an inanimate object: 'mighty' or 'noble ruin(s)' (pp. 346, 351), 'cold ashes' (p. 351), a 'woman's toy' (p. 349); as dead (p. 355); as a savage: 'commoner of Nature' (p. 351); as madman (p. 354); eunuch: 'unmanned' (p. 349); slave (p. 356); as 'shadow of an emperor' (p. 351); as 'more pitiful' than 'praying virgins' (p. 349); as an ex-man: 'I have been a man' (p. 354), 'the blank' of the man 'he was' (p. 349). Later in the play, as already noted, he repeatedly appears as an infant.[13] In Act V Alexas, echoing the animal imagery of Act I, says of Antony's heart that it

> was never lost, but started off
> To jealousy, love's last retreat and covert;
> Where it lies hid in shades, watchful in silence,
> And listening for the sound that calls it back. (p. 419)

and Cleopatra hears his last words as 'the notes of dying swans' (p.

---

[12] See Maynard Mack's 'Introduction,' pp. liii-lxiii, to his edition of *An Essay on Man* (London, 1950), vol. III, i, of the Twickenham edition of Pope's poems.
[13] Most notably in an image Muir ridicules (Muir, p. 141):

> O Cleopatra!
> O Dolabella! how could you betray
> This tender heart, which with an infant fondness
> Lay lulled betwixt your bosoms, and there slept,
> Secure of injured faith?
>
> (Act IV, p. 414)

The image is certainly grotesque, but not nonfunctional.

432). The less-than-man imagery of Act I is also echoed later. Dolabella in Act III challenges Antony to receive Octavia and the children with the formula: 'if you confess a man' (p. 386). Antony himself at one point in Act IV intends 'to recollect what's left of man within' (p. 411), and in Act V sees himself as dreamer (p. 425) and murderer (p. 426). Images of contraction are part of the same pattern. Antony is 'shrunk from the vast extent of all his honours,' says Ventidius in Act I (p. 349); 'The place thou pressest on thy mother earth Is all thy empire now,' says Antony of himself shortly afterwards (p. 351); a few lines further on he foresees the time when he will have 'contracted in thy narrow urn, Shrunk to a few cold ashes' (p. 351); and in Act II he complains that because of Cleopatra

> The world fell mouldering from my hands each hour,
> And left me scarce a grasp—(p. 371)

It may be objected to many of these images that their specific imagistic content is not really functional in any larger design, that the fearful deer(?) and the dying swans above share only a vague and general classification and thus fail to connect in the listener's or reader's mind, serving only local decorative or illustrative purposes, in the manner of the detachable Homeric simile-metaphor. The psychology of perceiving images in literature hardly lends itself to exact study, and criticism varies in the rules by which it counts or does not count a given image a member of a larger pattern,—if it works by rules at all. A pragmatic attitude seems soundest in these matters. One important way in which one critic is professionally better than another is his superior success in convincing his audience that the patterns he discovers in the literary work really exist. And to the extent critical analysis can make good a case for calling Dryden's imagery in *All for Love* miscellaneous, his imagery must be said to perform less finely than Shakespeare's. Still, the pervasive complex of less-or-other-than-man images in the play generates a cumulative force of crucial thematic significance, most strongly felt in Act I, perhaps, and even there felt to be coherent in terms of fairly broad classes of imagery rather than of bright, concrete detail, but never wholly inoperative. Since Dryden's dramatic strategy would not permit any good and likable character to speak the cause of reason against the lovers' unreason (hence Ventidius' suicide), the glorification of unreason would have to be tempered in some other way, lest it appear simply foolishly sentimental. The imagery of Antony as no man, ex-man, infant and man *manqué*, to which every reader bred in the Renaissance tradition of Christian humanism would respond, does the job.

For the cause of reason *is* in unattractive hands. They are not, as we just noted, Ventidius'; he is the representative of blunt virtue and soldierly honor rather than of reason. Alexas, the 'half-man' of self-conscious intellect, recognizes in Ventidius his own foil:

> This downright fighting fool, this thick-skulled hero,
> This blunt, unthinking instrument of death,
> With plain dull virtue has outgone my wit. (Act III, p. 391)

Octavia is neither attractive nor evil, but neither does she represent reason—rather self-righteous marital virtue. More than anything else she strikes one as an unhumorous version of 'the wife' of Restoration comedy, 'that thing, That dull insipid lump, without desires, And without power to give them,' (p. 363), as Cleopatra, like a female Dorimant, defines her breed. Dolabella, who is first brought into the play as an ally of Ventidius in the anti-Cleopatra campaign, quickly yields the claims of friendship to those of love, succumbing once again to Cleopatra's charms and—reluctant—wiles. And though he quickly repents of his weakness (if only after he sees that he will not succeed in any case) and seeks to regain Antony's trust and friendship and thus saves his character as a nice young man in our eyes, we hardly feel we have been observing a man of reason. Serapion believes in supernatural omens and, besides, has other functions in the play than to be part of the passion-reason conflict. The other named characters—Myris, Charmion, and Iras—obviously do not count in this connection.

That leaves only Alexas as reason's spokesman and exemplar among the on-stage characters. And Alexas, despite his apparently genuine Egyptian patriotism, is also the play's least attractive character, tarnished as he is by cowardice, envy, selfishness, and fawning hypocrisy.[14] And rather than being proof of Dryden's confused attitude to reason in this play, Alexas' being a eunuch is very much to its main point. If the role of reason is felt to be ambivalent it is largely due to the implications of impotence and sterility that cling to its sole devotee. Alexas' sexlessness is one of the play's major symbols. It is in this context that his soliloquy on death should be read:

> O that I less could fear to lose this being,
> Which, like a snowball in my coward hand,
> The more 'tis grasped, the faster melts away.
> Poor reason! what a wretched aid art thou!
> For still, in spite of thee,
> These two long lovers, soul and body, dread
> Their final separation. Let me think:
> What can I say, to save myself from death? (p. 423)

---

[14] Sale thinks Alexas unfairly maligned, by fellow characters and readers alike. See his notes to the play, *passim*.

His words echo in our ears as, a few minutes later, Antony, as a result of Alexas' 'thinking,' throws himself on his sword, exclaiming:

> death, for aught I know,
> Is but to think no more. Here's to be satisfied. (p. 430)

But further: given his sexual status it is appropriate for Alexas to refer to his 'being' in the figure of a snowball. The intrinsic worthlessness of the snowball—any snowball—anticipates the worthlessness of that physical being which the lovers so gladly will soon forego. And just as the reason that had honor, power, friendship, virtue, and life on its side is incapable of keeping Antony and Cleopatra apart, so Alexas here admits to reason's impotence when it argues a kind of stoical fearlessness in the face of death: for all his philosophy, body and soul *will* dread their separation. The first half of the soliloquy implies life's worthlessness considered merely as physical existence. The second half implies its value when it is regarded as a state of lovers' union. In fairness to the Muir position, however, it must be admitted that Dryden's imagery in *All for Love* does not often function so richly and subtly as here. And even here—one notices with chagrin—the pattern of values would have seemed more definite and manifest if the reference to Antony as 'unmanned' (p. 349) were gone and if Dryden's withholding man's full status also from Octavius, the 'boy Caesar' (pp. 376, 379, 424), did not blurringly impinge upon the complex of images that gives us Antony, passion's champion-victim, as something less than man, including infant. It is indeed my point here that Muir overstated his strictures on Dryden's imagery; a considerable number of them interact meaningfully. But I am not prepared to call Dryden's way with functional iterative imagery either sure or consistent.

But such a claim could be substantiated by the imagery of the death scene in Act V. Here Dryden successfully manages plot and both scenic and verbal image in a collaboration that achieves the triumph of heroic passion over unheroic reason.

> Ten years' love,
> And not a moment lost, but all improved
> To the utmost joys,—what ages have we lived? (p. 432)

says the dying Antony, voicing sovereign Love's traditional triumph over time, the world's measure of existence. Carefully Dryden arranges the final tableau for Love's supreme victory: the lovers' assumption of royal command of the world they lose. Cleopatra lays claim to the name of wife in defiance of those 'Roman laws' which Octavius survives to enforce.[15] The dead Antony is crowned with the victor's laurel.

---

[15] Is it too much to ask here that we forget her earlier scorn for a wife?

Cleopatra seats herself beside him, decked with the 'ensigns of . . . pomp and royalty,' bride and queen at once.

> I claim this place;
> For I must conquer Caesar too, like him,
> And win my share of the world. (p. 434)

Iras speaks of Cleopatra as 'our great queen and mistress,' and in one of Dryden's felicitous phrasal borrowings from Shakespeare the theme of queenship triumphant is repeated:

> *Serap.* 'Twas what I feared.—
> Charmion, is this well done?
> *Char.* Yes, 'tis well done, and like a queen, the last
> Of her great race: (p. 436)

Love's triumph is complete. Alexas, Reason's half-man, appears bound, to witness the dead lovers in their state and to speak a kind word for their death. He is, we learn, to appear in Octavius' triumphal procession in Rome, and though Serapion's reasons for considering him a 'villain' are none too clear, he is obviously a sorry substitute in the part originally intended for Cleopatra. The queen has escaped with her lover to walk 'hand in hand' 'in groves below,' while

> Whole troops of lovers' ghosts shall flock about us,
> And all the train be ours. (p. 432)

leaving Caesar to 'rule' the world, which, in Serapion's words, is subject to 'human chance' and 'all the storms of fate.'

Serapion's part is small but not unimportant. He both opens and closes the play. His account of the 'portents and prodigies,' in the first scene of the play, is, significantly, an account of omens of excess: the overflowing Nile, a whirlwind that opens vaults—clearly fit harbingers of the tragic events that follow and that reach their climax in Cleopatra's open 'monument' of burial. And in retrospect, the image of the dead Ptolemy, 'the boy-king' who 'Reared his inglorious head' (p. 344), is seen as a precursor of Octavius, another inglorious 'boy' ruler, whose base spirit haunts the play.

But not only is Serapion the speaker of meaningful images in the opening scene of the play; to him also falls the conventional task of taking charge in the final scene, after the death of the tragic protagonists. By tradition, this function belonged to the play's highest ranking surviving character—here obviously Octavius. It is all the more significant, then, that the task is *not* Octavius'. Throughout the play we have sensed this cool Caesar as a growing pressure on the lovers' realm of passion—the pressure of disciplined rationality: cold, calculating, shrewd, cautious, massive, inexorable, until now, in the last moments of the play, we all but hear his measured steps approaching love's inner sanctum. But he never enters. Reason may win the world, but we never see it take command. It is good theater but even better literature to keep Octavius off the stage till the end. This is the lovers' play.

And Serapion's task of taking charge entails another traditional function: that of speaking the lovers' epitaph. Its opening lines represent the play's imagistic climax in a key paradox:

> See how the lovers sit in state together,
> As they were giving laws to half mankind! (p. 436)

It is as if the 'all' the lovers lose for their passion does *not* comprise sway of 'the world.'

To read this ending as an advocacy of heedless romantic passion in defiance of reason, prudence, honor, and virtue would be not only to parody hideously the didactic theory of literature, but also to distort drastically, by way of over-simplification, the ultimate meaning of the play. What Dryden accomplishes in *All for Love* is a serious questioning, in terms of a mood of pathos, a plot whose moving force is flux of feeling, and imagery of cold reason and love triumphant, of Octavius' and Alexas' kind of reason. He questions it as a complete and exclusive guide to the conduct—not of the safe, but of the fulfilled, life. This is an anticipation of the state of mind in which, in *Religio Laici*, a few years later, in the name of fideism and philosophical scepticism,[16] Dryden limited (but, we should note, did not renounce) reason:

> Dim, as the borrow'd beams of Moon and Stars
> To *lonely, weary, wandring* Travellers,
> Is *Reason* to the *Soul:*

The play celebrates the passional life, the poem religious faith, but the questioning of reason's supremacy and efficacy as a guide to the good life is common to both.

Dryden's imitation of *Antony and Cleopatra* obviously represents a reduction of his model on all counts: in scope of action, in vigor and range of characterization, in subtlety, intensity, and unity of imagery of speech and event. The reduction was partly deliberate—his theme was an ennobling variant of the standard neoclassical theme of the destructiveness of passion, and his manner not cynical-sensual like

16 See Louis I. Bredvold, *The Intellectual Milieu of John Dryden* (Ann Arbor, Mich., 1934) and Miss Hartsock's essay cited above. Miss Hartsock's emphasis on Hobbesian influence on Dryden is meant as a corrective supplement to Bredvold's discussion of Dryden's relationship to seventeenth-century traditions of philosophical scepticism.

Shakespeare's but pathetic and compassionate—and partly the result of Dryden's being the lesser poet, even, for all his superior tidiness, the lesser dramaturge. And yet, his version of the legend does not simply shrink Shakespeare's heroic lovers to the requirements of a lachrymose bourgeoisie. His Antony is made of more pliant stuff than Shakespeare's, a passive weeper where Shakespeare's rails and fights, and there are moments in Acts IV and V in which Dryden's Cleopatra appears to have strayed from the heroine's part in some early version of *Love's Last Shift*. But Passion's final paradoxical triumph over Reason takes place in a moment of heroic grandeur, pity ceding to passion, sentiment to magnitude, as the imperial lovers, 'giving laws to half mankind,' extend their romantic dominion to 'late posterity.' In this moment of Passion's apotheosis life lived and lost recklessly and emotionally is felt to be life lived not foolishly and viciously but bravely, freely, and fully. It is a theme woven into Dryden's whole design. And so, in emulating the divine Shakespeare, Dryden, one would like to think, may well have felt he had earned the right to number himself one in the estimable band of imitators who can say of themselves that 'we . . . are not without glory even in our overthrow.'

All for Love

by Arthur C. Kirsch

All for Love preserves many of the features of Dryden's rhymed plays. It is peripatetic in structure; and it purports to deal with heroic issues: Antony's love is presented in the words of one recent critic, as "a suitable enterprise for a hero." [1] As in *Aureng-Zebe,* however, the heroism of *All for Love* is subverted at every turn by sentimental effects which emphasize not the heroic glory of love, but its domesticity and compassion. In *All for Love* Dryden develops the sentimental tendencies of his earlier plays and responds, as we shall see, to the challenge that had been offered by the passionate drama of his young and highly popular contemporaries, Lee and Otway.

Dryden gives some indication of his sentimental intentions in the preface, where he remarks that he designed the play "to work up the pity [of the original story] to a greater heighth . . ." and criticizes himself for introducing Octavia, who by "the dividing of pity" between her and Cleopatra, "like the cutting of a River into many Channels, abated the strength of the natural stream." He is even more explicit in the prologue. The author, he writes:

> . . . *fights this day unarm'd; without his Rhyme.*
> *And brings a Tale which often has been told;*
> *As sad as* Dido's; *and almost as old.*
> *His Heroe, whom you Wits his Bully call,*
> *Bates of his mettle; and scarce rants at all:*
> *He's somewhat lewd; but a well-meaning mind;*
> *Weeps much; fights little; but is wond'rous kind.*
> *In short, a Pattern, and Companion fit,*
> *For all the keeping Tonyes of the Pit,*
> *I cou'd name more: A Wife, and Mistress too;*
> *Both (to be plain) too good for most of you:*
> *The Wife well-natur'd, and the Mistress true.*

All for Love *from* Dryden's Heroic Drama *(Princeton, N. J.: Princeton University Press, 1965) by Arthur C. Kirsch, pp. 128-33. Copyright © 1965 by Princeton University Press. Reprinted by permission of the publisher.*

[1] Waith, *The Herculean Hero,* p. 200. Waith's interpretation of *All for Love* differs markedly from mine; see *ibid.,* pp. 188-200.

Despite the evident banter and exaggeration of these lines, Dryden seems to be informing his audience that they should expect not only new versification but new conceptions of character. The play itself bears out his warning. Octavia is introduced as the symbol of the family. Although she speaks in the name of the Roman empire, her role in the play is really defined by her domestic relationships: as a wife, as a mother, and as a sister. Like Melisinda she is an abused wife, and like her also she is loyal and "well-natur'd"; she leaves Antony only after she has exacted from him, from Ventidius, from Dollabella, and from the audience, a full measure of the thrills of domestic piety. Her reconciliation scene with Antony is a paradigm of sentimental drama. She enters, "*leading* Antony's *two little Daughters*," and she and Antony stage a brief debate in what appears to be the old style, "a strife of sullen Honour." But she confesses her love, Antony has to stifle a tear, and as Antony himself makes clear, the debate shifts from honor to pity. "Pity," he says, "pleads for *Octavia;* | But does it not plead more for Cleopatra?" Ventidius answers that "Justice and Pity both plead for *Octavia,*" and Antony admits to a "distracted Soul." The maudlin resolution of the scene is worth quoting at length:

> *Octav.* Sweet Heav'n, compose it.
> Come, come, my Lord, if I can pardon you,
> Methinks you should accept it. Look on these;
> Are they not yours? Or stand they thus neglected
> As they are mine? Go to him, Children, go;
> Kneel to him, take him by the hand, speak to him,
> For you may speak, and he may own you too,
> Without a blush; and so he cannot all
> His Children: go, I say, and pull him to me,
> And pull him to yourselves from that bad Woman.
> You, *Agrippina,* hang upon his arms;
> And you, *Antonia,* clasp about his waste:
> If he will shake you off, if he will dash you
> Against the Pavement, you must bear it, Children;
> For you are mine, and I was born to suffer.
>   (*Here the Children go to him, etc.*)
>   *Ven.* Was ever sight so moving! Emperor!
>   *Dolla.* Friend!
>   *Octav.* Husband!
>   *Both Childr.* Father!
>   *Ant.* I am vanquish'd: take me,
> *Octavia;* take me, Children; share me all.
>   (*Embracing them.*)
> I've been a thriftless Debtor to your loves,

And run out much, in riot, from your stock;
But all shall be amended.
   Octav.   O blest hour!
   Dolla. O happy change!
   Ven.   My joy stops at my tongue,
But it has found two channels here for one,
And bubbles out above.
   Ant. to Octav. This is thy Triumph; lead me where thou wilt;
Ev'n to thy Brother's Camp.
   Octav.   All there are yours.

                        (pp. 37, 39, 40-41; V, 389-91) [2]

Dryden may have had reason to regret the division of pity which
such a scene caused, but its tears and sentiment are not inconsistent
with the affective emphasis in the rest of the play. Cleopatra, though
somewhat less masochistic than Octavia, is similarly domesticated and
sentimentally self-indulgent. In one speech she complains that "Nature
meant" her to be "A Wife, a silly harmless household Dove, / Fond
without art; and kind without deceit" (p. 47; V, 399), and although
these lines can be misleading out of context, they do nonetheless describe her wishes accurately. In spirit, if not in name, she is indeed a
suffering wife: utterly "true," as Dryden describes her in the prologue,
utterly without the sexual independence which characterizes the heroines of Dryden's earlier plays. "She dotes, / She dotes . . . on this
vanquish'd Man" (p. 3; V, 346), Alexas remarks, and she herself be-
wails "the curse / Of doting on, ev'n when I find it Dotage!" (p. 63;
V, 418). Although she proclaims the heroism of this dotage and its
simplicity (her love, she insists, is "plain, direct and open"), the play's
emphasis is not upon the magnanimity of her fidelity but upon the
hardships which she must endure because of it. Her major scenes are
those in which she must face the loss of Antony, and in all them she
proves herself by the sincerity of her grief. When Dollabella pretends
that Antony has cast her off unkindly, *"she sinks quite down"* on the
stage (p. 50; V, 402), and after her encounter with Octavia, she exits
to a "solitary Chamber,"

                 . . . to take alone
       My fill of grief:
       There I till death will his unkindness weep
       As harmless Infants moan themselves asleep.

                            (p. 44; V, 395)

---

[2] The texts of the quotations from Dryden are always those of the first edition,
but reference is also made to the Scott-Saintsbury edition of his works. Thus the
reference pp. 37, 39, 40-41; V, 389-91 means that the text of the quotation is on
pages 37, 39, 40-41 of the first edition of *All for Love* and may also be consulted
in volume V, pp. 389-91 of the Scott-Saintsbury edition.

Cleopatra is heroic, worthy of Antony, not because she is a queen and a woman infinite in variety, but because she suffers and deserves pity, as she herself is quick to point out to Octavia:

> Yet she who loves him best is *Cleopatra*.
> If you have suffer'd, I have suffer'd more.
> You bear the specious Title of a Wife,
> To guild your Cause, and draw the pitying World
> To favour it: the World contemns poor me;
> For I have lost my Honour, lost my Fame,
> And Stain'd the glory of my Royal House,
> And all to bear the branded Name of Mistress.
> There wants but life, and that too I would lose
> For him I love.
>
> (p. 44; V, 394)

Antony, too, is willing to sacrifice all for love, and in him the accent on suffering and compassion is even more marked. Not "altogether wicked, because he could not then be pitied," he is as different from the heroical hero of Dryden's earlier plays as he is from Shakespeare's hero. Indecisive, and the constant prey of conflicting sentiments, he is thrown by the successive pleas of Ventidius, Octavia, Dollabella, and Cleopatra into alternating postures of grief and hope; and his ability to assume such postures with extravagance and tears becomes the final measure of his heroism. Early in the play Ventidius accords Antony the credentials of the earlier heroes: a "vast soul" and Herculean divinity:

> Methinks you breath
> Another Soul: Your looks are more Divine;
> You speak a Heroe, and you move a God.
>
> (pp. 5, 14; V, 347, 359)

But the context of Ventidius' praise is a scene which exploits precisely those qualities in Antony which make him less than a god: his compassionate sensibilities, and his "tender heart." Antony gives in to Ventidius in this scene and agrees to resume the duties of his empire less to assert his glory than to demonstrate his affection for his friend. He hugs Ventidius and weeps with him:

> Sure there's contagion in the tears of Friends:
> See, I have caught it, too. Believe me, 'tis not
> For my own griefs, but thine.
>
> (p. 9; V, 353)

His relationship with Cleopatra, though more complicated, is similarly sentimental; heroic issues again are essentially excuses for the exercise of emotion. Antony claims often that Cleopatra "deserves / More Worlds than I can lose" (p. 12; V, 357), but when the play begins he has already effectively lost the world and we see him *"walking with a disturb'd Motion,"* and shortly afterwards, lying prostrate upon the stage. Antony proves his worth as a lover much as Cleopatra does, not by giving away worlds which are no longer in his power to give, but by showing his capacity for sympathy and suffering. He can almost always be reduced to tears by his friends and by her—"One look of hers, would thaw me into tears," he tells Dollabella, "And I should melt until I were lost agen." (p. 45; V, 395)—and in virtually every situation in which we see him on stage, his grandeur is shown by the enormity of his distress. No longer a conqueror, a family man rather than a superman, Antony is the hero of a play which exalts the man of feeling, the man who *"Weeps much; fights little; but is wond'rous kind."* [3]

[3] The weeping of the men in *All for Love* is especially conspicuous. Antony cries three times onstage (pp. 9, 39, 62-3; V, 353, 388, 417) and once his "falling tear" is reported (p. 17; V, 362). Dollabella cries when Antony exiles him (pp. 62-3; V, 417) and even Ventidius cries twice, once in grief for Antony (p. 9; V, 352) and once in joy over Antony's family reunion (p. 41; V, 390).

PART TWO

Viewpoints

Hazelton Spencer

There are those who see technical excellence in the play. It seems to me more apparent than real. There is a unity of action, certainly, but it is of the most artificial kind. As a matter of fact, the play is a series of confrontations between Antony and Ventidius, Antony and Alexas, Antony and Cleopatra, Antony and Octavia, Octavia and Cleopatra, etc., etc. One scene does not grow out of another, or out of characterization; the action is essentially arbitrary with the dramatist, not spontaneous with the characters. And the style is rarely good enough to redeem this defect, as it so often is redeemed in Racine.

Characterization (this is the play's most grievous fault) has been dedicated to the great principle of consistency. Antony is the merest sentimentalist; Cleopatra's degradation at Dryden's hands is even more pitiful. Shakespeare's great psychological portrait of the queen and woman is turned to the wall in favor of the puppet of a ruling passion. The complex human being, with her infinite variety, gives place to a lay figure of Woman in Love.

The unity of place is likewise achieved by arbitrary measures; the poet does not even trouble to excuse his characters for appearing so promptly and so pat. They saunter in and saunter out from the four quarters of the Mediterranean world, as if their leisure hours were habitually passed in wandering up and down the streets of Alexandria. Poetic justice is not respected except in the death of the hero and heroine. Violence on the stage is permitted in the deaths of five of the characters. Of comedy, even of ironic comedy, there is none; there is no wishing her joy of the worm.

The influence of the heroic drama is powerful in this play, as it is in Dryden's alteration of *Troilus and Cressida*. The heroics not infrequently pass over into the extreme absurdities of that derided form, yet the passion is rarely wild or indecorous. Even the diction, the best thing in the play, is for the most part smooth and flowing. There is rant in profusion, but the daring homeliness, which makes so many of Shakespeare's metaphors so impressive, is never indulged in. As Pro-

From "Dryden's Adaptations" in Shakespeare Improved (Cambridge, Mass.: Harvard University Press, 1927) by Hazelton Spencer, pp. 220-21. Copyright 1927 by the President and Fellows of Harvard College. Reprinted by permission of Harvard University Press.

fessor Saintsbury points out, there is nothing like Cleopatra's

> Peace, peace:
> Dost thou not see my Baby at my breast,
> That suckes the Nurse asleepe?

which, he continues, "no poet save Shakespeare since the foundation of the world, would or could have written."

Judged by what he conceived a tragedy ought to be and by what he tried to accomplish with his source, the author of *All for Love* achieved a remarkable *tour de force*. No one in his senses desires to deny to the great name of Dryden one scruple of the praise that such an accomplishment deserves. But our admiration for its author's genius does not oblige us to like this play or, for more than a moment in the fifth act, to believe in it.

T. S. Eliot

As for the verse of 'All for Love' and the best of Dryden's blank verse in the other plays in which he used it, it is to me a miracle of revivification. I think that it has more influence than it has had credit for; and that it is really the norm of blank verse for later blank verse playwrights. How Dryden could have escaped so completely the bad influence of the last followers of Shakespeare, with their dissolution of rhythm nearly into prose, and their worn-out wardrobe of imagery, is as wonderful as his superiority to, and difference from, the other schools of verse, that of the Senecal poets, and D'Avenant to whom he was somewhat indebted. I will hazard here an heretical and contestable opinion; that later blank verse dramatists have written better verse when they wrote more like Dryden (whether they were aware of it or not), and worse blank verse when they were conscious of Shakespeare.

From "Dryden the Dramatist" by T. S. Eliot. From The Listener, *V, No. 119 (April 22, 1931), p. 681. Copyright 1931 by T. S. Eliot. Reprinted by permission of Mrs. T. S. Eliot.*

F. R. Leavis

Dryden's Antony couldn't have sat in the market-place whistling to the air; his dignity wouldn't have permitted it. Or rather, to ask whether he could or not is to introduce a criterion of reality in the

From "'Antony and Cleopatra' and 'All for Love': A Critical Exercise" by F. R. Leavis. From Scrutiny, *V, No. 2 (September, 1936), pp. 165-67. Copyright 1936 by F. R. Leavis. Reprinted by permission of the author.*

presence of which he doesn't exist. His Cleopatra couldn't have hopped
in the public street, or anywhere. His tragic *personæ* exist only in a
world of stage-postures; decorum gone, everything is gone. Shakespeare's have a life corresponding to the life of the verse; the life in
them is, in fact, the life of the verse. Correspondingly, his poem as
drama—in situation, larger rhythm, cumulative effect—has an actuality,
a richness and a depth in comparison with which it becomes absurd
to discuss Dryden's play as tragedy. It is, of course, understood that in
a sustained reading Shakespeare's poetry conveys an organization such
as cannot be examined in an extracted passage.

. . . About Dryden's rendering there is nothing to say except that it
has none of the poetic—and that is, we have seen, the dramatic—life
of the original. It is accomplished verse, and verse that lends itself to
stage-delivery, but it is hardly poetry. It is not poetry, in the sense
that it is not the product of a realizing imagination working from
within a deeply and minutely felt theme. Dryden is a highly skilled
craftsman, working at his job from the outside. The superior structure
with which his play is credited as a theater-piece is a matter of workmanship of the same external order as is represented by his verse. He
aims at symmetry, a neat and obvious design, a balanced arrangement
of heroic confrontations and 'big scenes.' The satisfaction he offers his
audience is that of an operatic exaltation and release from actuality,
a ballet-like completeness of pattern, and an elegantly stylized decorum.

It may, of course, be urged on his behalf that he does not offer a
poetic concentration comparable with Shakespeare's, but exhibits his
strength only to the more inclusive view, in more spacious relations,
so that it is peculiarly unfair to represent him . . . in a short passage.
To this it must be replied that his quality is still the quality of his
verse, his virtue still a matter of taste, judgment, and workmanship.
The point may be fairly coercively made by an observation regarding
what, in Dryden's verse, takes the place of the life of metaphor and
imagery in Shakespeare's. What we find, when we can put a finger
on anything, is almost invariably either a formal simile, or a metaphor
that is a simile with the 'like' or the 'as' left out. The choice is so wide
and the showing so uniform that illustration must be random:

> He could resolve his mind, as Fire does Wax,
> From that hard rugged Image, melt him down,
> And mould him in what softer form he pleas'd.

> And yet the Soul, shut up in her dark Room,
> Viewing so clear abroad, at home sees nothing;
> But, like a Mole in Earth, busie and blind,
> Works all her folly up and casts it outward
> To the Worlds open view.

the least kind word, or glance,
You give this Youth, will kindle him with Love.
Then, like a burning Vessel set adrift,
You'll send him down amain before the wind,
To fire the Heart of jealous Antony.

With fiery Eyes, and with contracted Brows,
He Coyn'd his Face in the severest stamp:
And fury shook his Fabrick like an Earthquake;
He heav'd for vent, and burst like bellowing Aetna,
In Sounds scarce humane . . .

I find your Breast fenc'd round from humane reach,
Transparent as a Rock of solid Chrsytal;
Seen through, but never pierc'd.
But I am made a shallow-forded Stream,
Seen to the Bottom: all my clearness scorn'd,
And all my Faults expos'd!

The structure, it will be seen, is always that of simple, illustrative, point-by-point correspondence. One analogy may give way to another, and so again, but the shift is always clean and obvious; there is never any complexity, confusion or ambiguity. When there is development, it is simple, lucid and rational.

This habit of expression manifests plainly the external approach, the predominance of taste and judgment. It is an approach equally apparent in the treatment of emotion in what are meant to be the especially moving places—as, for instance, in the scene in which Octavia and the children are loosed upon Antony:

Antony: Oh, Dollabella, which way shall I turn?
I find a secret yielding in my Soul;
But Cleopatra, who would die with me,
Must she be left? Pity pleads for Octavia
But does it not plead more for Cleopatra?

. . . .

(Here the Children go to him, etc.)

Ventidius: Was ever sight so moving! Emperor!
Dollabella: Friend.
Octavia: Husband!
Both Children: Father!
Antony: I am vanquished: take me,
Octavia; take me, Children; share me all.
(Embracing them).

————The emotion doesn't emerge from a given situation realized in its concrete particualrity; it is stated, not presented or enacted. The explicitness is of the kind that betrays absence of realization.

B. Ifor Evans

It is clear from the prefatory verses to *Aureng-Zebe* that Dryden was growing tired of the composition of these grandiose heroic tragedies in rhymed verse. There was further in the 'seventies a change of taste that led back towards the more varied and real world of Shakespearean and Stuart tragedy. That Dryden himself had deeply admired these earlier authors appears almost everywhere in his critical work. It is true that during the period of his obsessive devotion to the heroic drama his affection was tempered sometimes with a belief that they were 'the giant race before the flood,' not fully aware of the elegance and refinements that a more modern age had introduced. Now in 1677 he returned to blank verse, and in *All for Love* wrote a play on the Antony and Cleopatra theme. He indulged in no slavish imitation of Shakespeare's play, though the composition shows again Dryden's admiration for Shakespeare. Dryden breaks down the widely distributed scenes of Shakespeare and brings the theme as close to the unity of action as its nature will permit. The picture of Antony is less generous than in Shakespeare, for the emphasis is on the very last phase, full of fretting and nerves and morbid suspicion. Nor has Cleopatra the 'infinite variety' that she once possessed. *Antony and Cleopatra* was the play in which Shakespeare approached the values of the Restoration stage most closely, for this is the only one of his mature tragedies in which love is made the dominant theme. *All for Love,* of all Dryden's plays, is the one in which the Restoration motives of love and honor are subordinated, and their place taken by suspicion and jealousy.

Abridged from A Short History of English Drama *by Sir Ifor Evans (London: MacGibbon and Kee Ltd., 1965), pp. 125-26. Copyright © 1965 by Sir Ifor Evans. Reprinted by permission of the author and publisher.*

Morris Freedman

Dryden's *All for Love* was published a year after he lavishly praised Milton in his preface to *The State of Innocence*. We should not be sur-

Abridged from "'All for Love' and 'Samson Agonistes,'" by Morris Freedman. From Notes and Queries CCI (December, 1956), pp. 514-17. Copyright © 1956 by Oxford University Press. Reprinted by permission of* Notes and Queries *and Oxford University Press.*

prised, then, to find that Dryden's appreciation of Milton extended to
his being influenced in *All for Love,* his blank verse drama modeled
on classical rules, by Milton's *Samson Agonistes* since, after all, a fore-
most critical and creative interest of Dryden was drama. Having been
so impressed by Milton's *Paradise Lost* as to try an adaptation of it,
it would have been equally, perhaps more, natural for him to respond
in not dissimilar manner to *Samson Agonistes.*

I should like to suggest that the verbal, thematic, and critical connections between *All for Love* and *Samson* are, in sum, so substantial
as to indicate that Dryden not only knew Milton well but was modifying Shakespeare through him.

Ventidius, to begin with him, retains little of the comradely good
fellowship of his original, Enobarbus. He has become, like the chorus
in *Samson,* a moral commentator on the action. His role as chorus is
suggested in the first scene of the play when he stands off and describes Antony (my italics):

> How sorrow shakes him!
> So, now the tempest tears him up by the roots,
> *And on the ground extends the noble ruin.*
> Lie there, thou shadow of an emperor;
> The place thou pressest on thy mother earth
> Is all thy empire now: now it contains thee;
> Some few days hence, and then 'twill be too large,
> When thou'rt contracted in thy narrow urn,
> Shrunk to a few cold ashes . . . (I, i) [1]

This recalls the similar description of Samson by the chorus:

> This, this is he; softly a while,
> Let us not break in upon him;
> O change beyond report, thought, or belief!
> *See how he lies at random, carelessly diffus'd.*
> With languish't head unpropt,
> As one past hope, abandon'd.
> And by himself given over . . . (115-21) [2]

Ventidius' choral function is further underscored by the striking
echoes from *Samson's* chorus in one of his speeches alone with Antony.

---

[1] *The Works of John Dryden,* ed. Walter Scott and George Saintsbury (Edinburgh,
1883), V, 351. The act and scene numbers in parentheses following the quotations
are for convenience in using another edition.

[2] *Milton's Complete Poems,* ed. Frank Allen Patterson (New York, 1939), p. 408.

Chorus

　　　　. . . or if better,
Counsel or Consolation we may
　　bring,

Salve to thy Sores, apt words have
　　power to swage
The tumors of a *troubl'd mind,*
And are as *Balm* to fester'd
　　wounds. (183-186) [3]

Ventidius

I would *bring balm* and pour it in
　　your *wounds,*
Cure your *distempered mind,* and

　　heal your fortunes. (I, 1) [4]

Not only are the themes identical here, but, as my italics indicate, the operative words that give the passages their same meaning.

More important than verbal correspondences are the thematic ones. Dryden's Antony is far closer to Milton's Samson, as is his Cleopatra to Dalila, and Ventidius (although only at times) to the chorus, than they are to their counterparts in Shakespeare's tragedy. I do not wish to overstress the connections, for Dryden, after all, was working with material that was only so far malleable; Dalila was married to Samson, an important consideration dramatically in Milton, while of course Cleopatra was not to Antony, an equally important dramatic point in Dryden.[5] But the tempestuous, mighty-spirited, mature lovers of Shakespeare were transformed by Dryden to resemble the far simpler, more predictable figures of Samson and Dalila.

Dryden's Antony is depicted, like Samson, as a man bereft of his masculine strength.

> Oh, she has decked his ruin with her love,
> Led him in golden bands to gaudy slaughter,
> And made perdition pleasing: She has left him
> The blank of what he was.
> I tell thee, eunuch, she has quite unmanned him. (I, i) [6]

The fatal flaw of Shakespeare's Antony is over-simplified to resemble Samson's uxoriousness. Dalila's overwhelming confidence that her touch alone ("Let me approach at least, and touch thy hand"—951) [7] would bring Samson back to her is echoed by Ventidius' passionate advice to Antony not to accept a gift from Cleopatra.

---

[3] *Ibid.,* p. 409.

[4] *Works,* V, 354-55.

[5] The Biblical Samson and Dalila, of course, were not married, which supports Dryden's parallel.

[6] *Works,* V, 349.

[7] *Complete Poems,* p. 424.

> Now, my best lord,—in honour's name, I ask you,
> For manhood's sake, and for your own dear safety,
> Touch not these poisoned gifts,
> Infected by the sender; touch them not . . . (II, i) [8]

A theme not pursued in Shakespeare so baldly is the insistence that Antony, like Samson, chose an alien woman, a recurrent motif in *Samson*.

> *Octavia:* I need not ask if you are Cleopatra;
> Your haughty carriage—
> *Cleopatra:* Shows I am a queen:
> Nor need I ask you, who you are.
> *Octavia:* A Roman:
> A name that makes and can unmake a queen.
> *Cleopatra:* Your lord, the man who serves me, is a Roman.
> *Octavia:* He was a Roman, till he lost that name,
> To be a slave in Egypt; but I come
> To free him thence. (III, i) [9]

The critical link between *All for Love* and *Samson* is perhaps more interesting even than the thematic and verbal similarities. In the preface to his drama Dryden announced that he desired "to be tried by the laws of my own country; for it seems unjust to me, that the French should prescribe here, till they have conquered." [10] He singled out the artist-critic as the one to follow in matters of art:

> Poets themselves are the most proper, though I conclude not the only critics. But till some genius, as universal as Aristotle, shall arise, one who can penetrate into all arts and sciences, without the practice of them, I shall think it reasonable that the judgment of an artificer in his own art should be preferable to the opinion of another man . . .[11]

It is to Milton that the above quotation from Dryden refers most specifically. Milton was the only writer of stature of the time (besides Dryden himself) who met the criterion for criticism that Dryden established here. He was a practising artist, and his *Samson,* in stated intention and fulfilment, comprised a body of English laws.

Not long after *All for Love,* in 1679, evidently pleased by his success in adhering to the classical rules, Dryden issued a new statement on tragedy, quite contradicting some of his earlier comments in the *Essay,* and echoing Milton's preface to *Samson Agonistes.*

[8] *Works,* V, 368.
[9] *Ibid.,* pp. 392-93.
[10] *Ibid.,* p. 331.
[11] *Ibid.*

Two different independent actions distract the attention and concern-
ment of the audience, and consequently destroy the intention of the
poet; if his business be to move terror and pity, and one of his actions
be comical, the other tragical, the former will divert the people, and
utterly make void his greater purpose. . . . This was the practice of the
Grecian stage.[12]

. . . the Poets error of intermixing Comic stuff with Tragic sadness and
gravity; or introducing trivial and vulgar persons, which by all judicious
hath bin counted absurd; and brought in without discretion, corruptly
to gratifie the people.[13]

All for Love would not have taken its present form without the
precedent of *Samson*. Dryden's other adaptations of Shakespeare were
not successful. *The Tempest* (1670) was Restoration low comedy;
Troilus and Cressida (1679) was, as Saintsbury said, a potboiler "which
might much better have been left unattempted." [14] *All for Love* bears
little relation to any heroic drama of the time. It was the first drama
after *Samson* to be written almost precisely according to the dictates
of Milton's preface: there is in it no admixture of comic and tragic,
no trivial and vulgar persons are introduced, the unities are observed,
and, except for couplets concluding acts in good Elizabethan fashion,
it is in a blank verse occasionally interspersed with short lines. If
Samson had not been written, or it had not been read by Dryden,
All for Love, if Dryden would have undertaken it at all, would certainly have fitted more closely into the Restoration pattern than it did.
The sea-change that Shakespeare's *Antony and Cleopatra* underwent
on its way to *All for Love* was in its passage through *Samson*.

H. Neville Davies

Dryden's debt to two English Cleopatra plays, Shakespeare's *Antony
and Cleopatra* and Daniel's *Tragedie of Cleopatra* has been widely
noted, but his debt to three other Cleopatra plays has remained un-

[12] *Works*, VI, 260-61. Noyes considers this passage to have been influenced by
Boileau, Rapin, Bossu, and Rymer. In view of Dryden's rejection in the preface to
All for Love both of French critics and of critics who were not also writers, Milton
as an English poet-critic would seem to have at least an equal claim with them
to inspiring the passage. See *The Poetical Works of Dryden,* ed. George R. Noyes
(Boston, 1950), xxxiv.
[13] *Complete Poems*, p. 405.
[14] George Saintsbury, *Dryden* (London, 1881), p. 60.
*From "Dryden's 'All for Love' and Thomas May's 'The Tragedie of Cleopatra
Queen of Ægypt'" by H. Neville Davies. From* Notes and Queries, *N. S. XII, No. 4
(April, 1965), pp. 140-41. Copyright © 1965 by Oxford University Press. Reprinted
by permission of* Notes and Queries *and Oxford University Press.*

noticed. Two of these, by Sedley, and by Fletcher and Massinger, I hope to consider in a further article. Here I shall consider the use Dryden made in his first act and perhaps also in his conclusion, of the third play, Thomas May's *The Tragedie of Cleopatra Queen of Ægypt* (acted 1626, published 1639 and 1654).

May begins the action of his play before the outbreak of war between Antonius and Octavius, and I assume that the Battle of Actium takes place at the end of Act II, at about the same time as the Egyptians are describing portents that have recently been seen. This passage corresponds in time to the beginning of *All for Love*, and seems to have inspired Dryden's opening scene.

In both plays the speakers of these passages are Egyptians, some of them being Egyptian priests, gathered at the Temple of Isis; and, in both, the alarming portents are related to Antony's defeat at Actium with the threat of consequent disaster for Egypt.

May acknowledges his sources throughout the play in a marginal gloss, and in this scene each portent is meticulously accompanied by a reference to Dio. Dryden's opening scene is clearly based on May's dramatization rather than Dio's account, or the similar account in Plutarch: for it is the dramatic framework, invented by May to contain the historical information, that Dryden copies. The historical information itself Dryden replaces by details more appropriate to the economy of his play, but which have no historical sanction. At this introductory point concern with special stylistic considerations militates against verbal borrowings, but a few words repeated by May occur singly in Dryden's concise version, especially ones that seem resonant or impressive without being demandingly explicit. (I will show that Dryden was here purposely writing, tongue in cheek, in the manner of a hack.) The whole of May's scene must be read to understand fully how Dryden has used it, but it is too long to quote. As the play is not available in a modern edition I will, however, quote a few extracts as examples of the extent to which verbal parallels exist between the two scenes. These examples are not intended as a proof of Dryden's indebtedness, though they may serve as corroborative evidence.

> (i)
> What dire portents sent from the wrathful Gods
> Threaten th'astonish'd world? What plagues are these
> Which in the skies prodigious face I read?
> Tumultuous Nature teems with monstrous births,
>> (*The T. of C.* Cl^r)
>
> . . . Italy and Rome it self are fill'd
> With prodigies;
>> (*The T. of C.* Cl^v)

But these portents do threaten Italy.

> *(The T. of C.* C2ʳ*)*

Cf.

Portents and Prodigies are grown so frequent,
That they have lost their Name.

> *(A. for L.* I. 1-2*)*

Here monstrous *Phocoe* panted on the Shore:

> *(A. for L.* I. 11*)*

(ii)

. . . now Sicilian Ætna nourishes
More horrid flames then usually it does,

> *(The T. of C.* C2ʳ*)*

And in the clouds that horrid noise was heard
That meeting armies make.

> *(The T. of C.* C3ʳ*)*

Cf.

On the cold pavement down I fell intranc'd
And so unfinish'd left the horrid scene.

> *(A. for L.* I. 30-31*)*

(iii)

The Gods avert it from our Ægypt's coast.

> *(The T. of* C. C1ᵛ*)*

> *Enter* Achoreus

Avert your anger, Gods, if all too late
Our prayers came not now.

> *(The T. of C.* C3ʳ*)*

Cf.

> *Enter* Alexas *behind them*

Avert these omens, Heav'n.

> *(A. for L.* I. 16*)*

Dryden has adapted May's material to his own particular needs. His version is considerably shorter than May's original: a compilation of portents and prodigies which becomes dull rather than horrific by excessive accumulation. Indeed, Dryden's first two lines seem to be not only a précis of May's lines but also a criticism of them. Brevity enables Dryden to use an extravagantly grand style, as bombastic as any purple passage typical of the heroic plays, whose style he claimed to have abandoned. In this way he establishes a dignified, tragic opening, abandoning it, like the opening 'grave' of a French overture, before it palls. But the heightened tone lingers even after we realize that Serapion, a typical butt of Dryden's anti-clerical satire, is a hysterical alarmist, and that Dryden is parodying the inflated heroic style as he uses it. The alliterative *p*'s seem to foreshadow the labial plosives of the "pomposo" opening of *Absalom and Achitophel* which Dryden wrote four years later. In both openings his intention is mock-heroic and anti-clerical. The educative function of Dryden's opening is another aspect which foreshadows his work as a satirist. By manipulating the audience to find the grand style ludicrous which at first it found impressive, Dryden is trying to create the taste by which the rest of the play may be appreciated.

W. Moelwyn Merchant

. . . The most striking change from Shakespeare is in the structure and duration of the scenes, particularly in the middle reaches of the play. For the cinematic *montage* of Shakespeare's brief scenes Dryden substitutes tableaux, the nearest approach of English drama to the statuesque of Racine. There are moments in Shakespeare's *Coriolanus* when we find a similar confrontation of classical ideals personified in persons who, for the moment, achieve symbolic dignity; Milton's *Samson Agonistes* is constructed wholly in this manner, with the opposition of single individuals in a conflict of principles. But Milton failed to assimilate the classical form to the theatric movement of western drama—if that was in any way his intention. But Dryden succeeds in the process, involving himself in so doing, in a pleasant irony of theater history. The flexibility of Jacobean setting enabled Shakespeare to maintain throughout the play the utmost subtlety in asserting the rival ideals of Rome and Alexandria against each other. This antithesis of the two cities is excluded by Dryden's adherence to the unity of place, and in this consistency of setting, Dryden goes beyond even the Jacobean convention of delocalisation; in a very real sense the stage itself, rather than a conventional Alexandria, is the conscious setting of the play. The successive entrances of Roman and Egyptian protagonists to confront each other make little if any demand on our feeling for locality; their points of view clash on an undifferentiated arena. This is of course not to say that décor was unimportant in *All for Love;* one significant detail, the elaborate death of Cleopatra, crowned and enthroned in dignity, is the regular *mise-en-scène* for the closing movement of the play both in Dryden's version and Shakespeare's.

Excerpted from "Shakespeare 'Made Fit'" by W. Moelwyn Merchant. From Restoration Theatre *edited by John Russell Brown and Bernard Harris (London: Edward Arnold (Publishers) Ltd., 1965), pp. 206-7. Copyright © 1965 by Edward Arnold (Publishers) Ltd. Reprinted by permission of the publisher.*

Chronology of Important Dates

	Dryden	General
1631	Dryden born August 9	Death of John Donne.
1642		Civil War Begins; theaters closed.
1649		Charles I executed.
1650	Dryden elected to a scholarship to Trinity College, Cambridge.	
1653		Cromwell made Protector.
1658		Cromwell dies.
1660	Dryden publishes *Astræa Redux* on the Restoration of Charles II.	Restoration of Charles II; Royal Society founded.
1662	Dryden elected fellow of the Royal Society.	
1663	Marries Lady Elizabeth Howard, sister of Sir Robert Howard.	
1666	*Annus Mirabilis* composed.	War with Holland; Great Fire of London.
1667		*Paradise Lost.*
1668	Dryden created Poet Laureate.	
1670	Dryden created Historiographer Royal.	
1671		Performance of *The Rehearsal,* in which Dryden and the heroic play are ridiculed.
1677	*All for Love* performed.	Publication of Thomas Rymer's *The Tragedies of the Last Age.*
1678		Popish Plot; beginning of the Exclusion Crisis.

1681 *Absalom and Achitophel* published.

Parliament meets at Oxford and is dissolved; ending of Exclusion Crisis.

1682 *Religio Laici* published.

1685 Dryden becomes a Roman Catholic.

Charles II dies; James II ascends the throne.

1687 *The Hind and the Panther* published.

1688 Dryden loses offices as Poet Laureate and Historiographer Royal.

William of Orange invades England; James II flees to France; William and Mary made joint monarchs.

1700 Dryden dies May 1.

Notes on the Editor and Contributors

BRUCE KING, editor of this volume, is Professor of English at the University of Lagos, Nigeria. His publications include *Dryden's Major Plays* and essays on Thoreau, Yeats, Graham Greene, jazz, and ballet, as well as seventeenth-century literature.

JOHN BAILEY is the author of many books, including *Poets and Poetry, The Claims of French Poetry, Shakespeare,* and *Dr. Johnson and His Circle.*

H. NEVILLE DAVIES is a Fellow of the Shakespeare Institute, University of Birmingham.

HAROLD E. DAVIS has published critical articles on Conrad and some of his own fiction. He is Professor of English at the University of New Mexico.

BONAMY DOBRÉE is a Professor Emeritus of Leeds University. His many publications include *Restoration Comedy, Restoration Tragedy, Rudyard Kipling* and *The Earlier Eighteenth Century*

T. S. ELIOT, poet and dramatist, published many works of criticism including a number of uncollected essays on Dryden. A volume in the Twentieth Century Views series, edited by Hugh Kenner, surveys Eliot's achievement.

EVERETT H. EMERSON has written a book on John Cotton and co-edited an edition of Milton's prose. He is Professor of English at the University of Massachusetts.

B. IFOR EVANS has written many books of criticism, including *Tradition and Romanticism* and *The Poetry of William Morris.* Sir Ifor has been Principal of Queen Mary College, The University of London, and Professor of English Language and Literature at The University of London.

MORRIS FREEDMAN is Professor of English at the University of Maryland. He has published *The Moral Impulse: Modern Drama from Ibsen to the Present.*

JEAN H. HAGSTRUM is author of *Samuel Johnson's Literary Criticism, William Blake, Poet-Painter,* and *The Sister Arts.* He is Professor of English at Northwestern University.

IRA JOHNSON has taught at the State College of Iowa and Le Moyne College.

ARTHUR C. KIRSCH presently teaches at the University of Virginia. He is the editor of *Literary Criticism of John Dryden.*

F. R. LEAVIS taught for many years at Cambridge and is Professor of English at the University of York, England. Among his influential books of criticism are *Revaluation, The Great Tradition,* and *The Common Pursuit.*

W. MOELWYN MERCHANT is Professor of English Language and Literature at the University of Exeter, and author of *Shakespeare and the Artist* and *Creed and Drama.*

KENNETH MUIR is King Alfred Professor of English Literature at the University of Liverpool. He has edited four of Shakespeare's plays and three volumes of Wyatt's poems and letters, as well as having written several books on Shakespeare and Milton.

OTTO REINERT has edited four drama anthologies and published articles on English and American literature and drama. He presently teaches at the University of Washington.

DAVID NICHOL SMITH, before his death, was Professor of English Literature at Oxford University. He is author of *Some Observations on Eighteenth Century Poetry.*

HAZELTON SPENCER, before his early death, was Professor of English at Washington State University and Johns Hopkins University.

NORMAN SUCKLING is Senior Lecturer in French at the University of Newcastle-upon-Tyne, England. His publications include *Fauré* and *Paul Valéry and the Civilized Mind.* His musical compositions have been performed in England and the United States.

EUGENE M. WAITH is Professor of English at Yale University. His publications include *The Pattern of Tragicomedy in Beaumont and Fletcher* and *The Herculean Hero.*

Selected Bibliography

The standard complete works of Dryden is the 1808 edition, edited by Sir Walter Scott and revised in 1882 by George Saintsbury. This is being superseded by the University of California edition of Dryden's work currently in progress. The standard biography is Charles E. Ward, *The Life of John Dryden* (Chapel Hill: University of North Carolina Press, 1961). For the dramas see Bruce King, *Dryden's Major Plays* (Edinburgh: Oliver and Boyd; New York: Barnes and Noble, 1966). Two good collections of essays are *Dryden: A Collection of Critical Essays,* ed. Bernard Schilling (Englewood Cliffs, N.J.: Prentice-Hall, 1963) and *Essential Articles for the Study of John Dryden,* ed. H. T. Swedenberg, Jr. (Hamden, Connecticut: Shoestring Press, 1966). For additional critical commentary on *All for Love,* see the articles by Moody E. Prior and R. J. Kaufmann in Schilling's collection, and Ruth Wallerstein's "Dryden and the Analysis of Shakespeare's Techniques" in the Swedenberg collection. Prior's essay can also be found in *The Language of Tragedy* (New York: Columbia University Press, 1947). Ruth Wallerstein's essay first appeared in the *Review of English Studies,* XIX (1943), 165-85.

Also useful is A. D. Hope's *"All for Love,* or Comedy as Tragedy" in *The Cave and The Spring* (Adelaide, Australia: Rigby, Ltd., 1965). D. T. Starnes examines various uses Dryden made of Shakespeare in "Imitation of Shakespeare in Dryden's *All for Love,"* in *Texas Studies in Literature and Language,* VI (1964), 39-46. Wallace Jackson discusses some of the problems faced by Augustan dramatists in "Dryden's Emperor and Lillo's Merchant" in *Modern Language Quarterly,* XXVI (1965), 536-44. Selma A. Zebouni's *Dryden: A Study in Heroic Characterization* (Baton Rouge: Louisiana State University Press, 1965) is unsympathetic to *All for Love,* but contains some good observations on the critical and literary background.